A History of Be

Alexei Sokolov

November 2025

Table of Contents

- **Introduction**
- **Chapter 1** The Dawn of History: Pre-Slavic Tribes and the Arrival of the Slavs
- **Chapter 2** The Principality of Polotsk: A Rival to Kyiv
- **Chapter 3** The Grand Duchy of Lithuania: A Union of Peoples
- **Chapter 4** The Golden Age: Culture and Law in the Grand Duchy
- **Chapter 5** The Polish-Lithuanian Commonwealth: A New Political Reality
- **Chapter 6** Religious Strife and the Rise of the Uniate Church
- **Chapter 7** The Deluge: War with Muscovy and the Decline of the Commonwealth
- **Chapter 8** The Partitions: The End of the Commonwealth and Russian Rule
- **Chapter 9** Life Under the Tsars: Russification and Resistance
- **Chapter 10** The Birth of a National Idea: The 19th Century Cultural Revival
- **Chapter 11** The Tumult of the Early 20th Century: World War I and the Struggle for Independence
- **Chapter 12** The Belarusian People's Republic: A Brief Glimmer of Statehood

- **Chapter 13** In the Soviet Crucible: The Formation of the BSSR
- **Chapter 14** The Interwar Years: Industrialization, Collectivization, and Repression
- **Chapter 15** The Great Patriotic War: Occupation and the Partisan Movement
- **Chapter 16** Post-War Reconstruction and Sovietization
- **Chapter 17** The Chernobyl Disaster and its Lingering Shadow
- **Chapter 18** The Path to Independence: The Late Soviet Period
- **Chapter 19** August 1991: The Declaration of a Sovereign State
- **Chapter 20** The Lukashenka Era: The Consolidation of Power
- **Chapter 21** Navigating East and West: Foreign Policy in the New Millennium
- **Chapter 22** Society and Identity in Post-Soviet Belarus
- **Chapter 23** The 2020 Protests: A Nation Awakens
- **Chapter 24** The Aftermath: Repression and International Isolation
- **Chapter 25** Belarus at a Crossroads: Challenges and Future Prospects

Introduction

To understand the story of Belarus is to understand a land caught in the crosscurrents of history. Situated in Eastern Europe, it is a nation defined as much by its geography as by the ambitions of its more powerful neighbors. A landlocked country, bordered by Russia, Ukraine, Poland, Lithuania, and Latvia, Belarus has for centuries been a thoroughfare for armies, a prize in imperial conflicts, and a space where cultures have clashed and mingled. This history is less a straightforward national narrative and more a study of the interplay of regional forces and their profound effects on the Belarusian people. Its very landscape, a generally flat terrain with vast tracts of marshland, forests, and thousands of lakes, offers few natural barriers, leaving it open to the tides of fortune, and misfortune, that have swept across the continent.

The name "Belarus" itself, translating to "White Rus'," is shrouded in theories, none definitive. The term *Belaya Rus'* might refer to the white clothing worn by the local Slavic population, or perhaps it designated the lands of the old Rus' that were not conquered by the Tatars in the 13th century. Another theory suggests a religious distinction, describing lands populated by early Christianized Slavs. The name first appears in medieval Latin and German texts, with the Englishman Sir Jerome Horsey being the first known to use "White Russia" in the late 16th century. Over time, the term became associated with the lands that form modern-day Belarus, though its historical ambiguity mirrors the nation's own complex and often contested identity.

The story of the Belarusian people begins with the migration of Slavic tribes into the region between the 6th and 8th centuries, where they settled and assimilated local Baltic and Finnic peoples. By the 9th century, these lands became part of the vast East Slavic state of Kievan Rus'. With the fragmentation of Kievan Rus' following the Mongol invasions of the 13th century, the Belarusian territories found a new political home within the expanding Grand Duchy of Lithuania. This period was formative, as the Belarusian lands retained a significant degree of autonomy, and the Old Belarusian language served as the official language of the Duchy for a time.

The subsequent union with the Kingdom of Poland created the Polish-Lithuanian Commonwealth, a vast and powerful state in which the Belarusian nobility became increasingly Polonized. This era was marked by cultural flourishing but also by religious strife and devastating wars, most notably the conflict with Muscovy in the 17th century known as "The Deluge," which began a long period of decline. The eventual partitions of the Commonwealth in the late 18th century erased it from the map, and the Belarusian lands were absorbed into the Russian Empire.

Life under the Tsars was a period of systematic Russification, where the Belarusian language was suppressed and its speakers officially classified as a variant of the Russian people. Despite this pressure, the 19th century witnessed the beginnings of a national cultural revival. The turmoil of the early 20th century provided a brief, flickering moment of statehood. Amid the chaos of World War I and the Russian Revolution, the Belarusian People's Republic was declared on March 25, 1918. This experiment in independence was short-lived, as the territory was soon divided between a resurgent Poland and the newly formed Soviet Union.

The Soviet era brought profound and often brutal transformations. As the Byelorussian Soviet Socialist Republic (BSSR), the nation experienced rapid industrialization and collectivization, but also the horrors of Stalinist purges that decimated its intellectual and political elites. World War II brought unparalleled devastation; military operations and the brutal Nazi occupation resulted in the loss of about a quarter of the population and the ruin of its economy. In the post-war years, Belarus was rebuilt and became a major industrial hub in the western USSR, a process that also intensified Russification. The Chernobyl nuclear disaster in 1986 cast a long and poisonous shadow over the southern part of the country, a catastrophe with which it still grapples.

The eventual dissolution of the Soviet Union saw Belarus declare its sovereignty in July 1990 and full independence in August 1991. The initial years of independence were a period of nation-building, marked by the restoration of national symbols and attempts to elevate the status of the Belarusian language. However, since the mid-1990s, the nation's path has been defined by the rule of its first and only president, Alexander Lukashenka, who has overseen a return to Soviet-era symbols and forged a close, though often complex, relationship with Russia.

This book traces the long and winding path of Belarusian history, from its earliest settlements to its current position at a geopolitical crossroads. It is a story of survival and resilience, of a culture and identity that have persisted through centuries of foreign domination and catastrophic conflict. It explores the formation of a state that has rarely known prolonged independence and a nation whose identity is a subject of ongoing debate. From the medieval principalities to the Grand Duchy, the Commonwealth, the Russian Empire, the Soviet crucible, and the complexities of the post-Soviet era, this history seeks to illuminate the forces that have shaped this fascinating and often misunderstood corner of Europe.

CHAPTER ONE: The Dawn of History: Pre-Slavic Tribes and the Arrival of the Slavs

Before the first Slavic voices echoed through the forests and marshes of what would become Belarus, the land was home to a succession of cultures known to us only through the patient work of archaeology. Human settlement in the region is ancient, with evidence of Upper Paleolithic inhabitants and widespread Neolithic remains. Long before the Slavs arrived, the territory was populated by a tapestry of peoples, primarily Baltic and Finno-Ugric tribes. Their world was one defined by the rhythms of the seasons, the hunt, and the rudimentary farming of forest clearings. These were not people who left written records; their stories are told in the fragments of pottery, the outlines of their fortified settlements, and the quiet reverence of their burial mounds, a silent testament to a world that existed for millennia before the great Slavic migrations reshaped the ethnic map of Eastern Europe.

Among the earliest groups identifiable by archaeologists is the Milograd culture, which flourished in what is now southern Belarus and northern Ukraine from roughly the 7th century BC to the 1st century AD. Named after a settlement in the Gomel region, the Milograd people were enigmatic; their precise ethnic identity remains a subject of scholarly debate, with theories pointing to them being either Baltic or perhaps even early proto-Slavs. They were contemporaries of the Scythians to the south, and their culture shows some influence from these nomadic warriors of the steppe. The Milograd people were succeeded by the Zarubintsy culture, which lasted from the 3rd century BC to the 1st century AD and occupied a similar territory along the Pripyat and Dnieper rivers. The Zarubintsy people were farmers who engaged in trade with the Black Sea region and were also influenced by the La Tène culture of the Celts to the west. Like their predecessors, they practiced cremation, burying the ashes of their dead in ceramic urns.

As the Iron Age progressed, the most dominant and widespread inhabitants of the Belarusian lands were various Baltic tribes. For centuries, this entire region was part of a vast Baltic-speaking world that stretched from the shores of the Baltic Sea far to the east, possibly reaching the vicinity of modern-day Moscow. These were not a unified people but a collection of related tribes. The most prominent in the territory of modern Belarus were the Dnieper Balts, a group whose existence is largely traced through the study of river names (hydronyms) which retain their Baltic linguistic roots. To the southwest, in the lands bordering present-day Poland and Lithuania, lived the Yotvingians, a formidable Western Baltic people known for their warrior culture. Archaeological finds in places like Mstislavl reveal the presence of Baltic settlements at the beginning of the millennium. These tribes lived in fortified hillforts, engaged in agriculture and animal husbandry, and were skilled artisans in pottery and metalwork.

The great turning point in the ethnography of the region began between the 6th and 8th centuries AD with the migration of Slavic peoples. Originating from a homeland that most scholars place in the area of Polesia, straddling modern-day southern Belarus and northern Ukraine, these tribes began a massive expansion across Eastern Europe. This was not a single, coordinated invasion led by kings and armies, but rather a gradual process of settlement by agricultural communities. These pagan, animistic people moved along the river systems, seeking out new lands for their slash-and-burn style of farming. As they moved into the territories of present-day Belarus, they encountered the established Baltic and Finnic populations. The interaction that followed was less a story of conquest and more one of slow assimilation and cultural fusion that would unfold over several centuries.

The Slavs who settled these lands were organized into large tribal unions, three of which would form the primary basis for the future Belarusian people. In the south, primarily in the marshy basin of the Pripyat River, lived the Dregovichi, or "people of the swamp." Their name, derived from an old word for "swamp," reflects the landscape they inhabited. They were first mentioned by the Byzantine Emperor Constantine Porphyrogenitus in the 10th century as the "Drougoubitai." The Dregovichi eventually established a political center at Turov, and their lands would later become the core of the Turov Principality. Their archaeological legacy includes remnants of agricultural settlements and distinctive burial mounds, or kurgans, where they initially practiced cremation.

To the east, along the Sozh River and its tributaries, settled the Radimichi. The *Primary Chronicle*, a key source for the history of the early East Slavs, offers a legendary origin for this tribe, claiming they "sprang from the Lyakhs" (an old term for Poles) and were named after a forefather called Radim. However, archaeological evidence suggests a more complex story, pointing to a mixed Slavic-Baltic origin for this tribal union. The Radimichi controlled strategically important river routes that connected them with the central regions of what would become Kievan Rus'. Over time, several towns emerged in their territory, including Gomel and Chechersk. Archaeologists can often identify Radimichi sites by the presence of distinctive seven-beamed temporal rings made of bronze or silver, a common feature of their female attire.

The largest and most influential of the Slavic tribal unions in the region were the Krivichi, who occupied the northern territories. Their domain was vast, covering the upper reaches of the Dnieper, Dvina, and Volga rivers, extending from the area around Pskov in the north down into central Belarus. This strategic position placed them astride the great trade route "from the Varangians to the Greeks," which linked Scandinavia with the Byzantine Empire, fostering trade and contact with Norse warrior-merchants. The name "Krivichi" may have Baltic roots, and like the Radimichi, they appear to have assimilated a significant local Baltic population. The major centers of the Krivichi were the ancient cities of Polotsk and Smolensk, as well as the important trade settlement of Gnezdovo. The Krivichi left behind a rich archaeological record, including the remains of settlements with evidence of skilled ironworking and jewelry making, as well as their characteristic long burial mounds.

The process by which the Slavs became the dominant population was gradual and complex. For several centuries, Baltic and Slavic communities coexisted, with the Neman and Western Dvina river basins remaining a mixed Baltic-Slavic area for a particularly long time. The Slavs possessed more advanced agricultural techniques and a more complex social organization, which likely contributed to their eventual demographic and linguistic dominance. Over time, the Baltic tribes were assimilated, leaving their mark in the names of rivers and places, and contributing to the genetic and cultural makeup of the emerging East Slavic groups. This prolonged period of interaction created a unique cultural substrate, a blend of Slavic and Baltic traditions that distinguished the people of this region from other East Slavs.

The economy of these early Slavic tribes was based primarily on subsistence agriculture, supplemented by hunting for furs, fishing, and beekeeping, which provided honey and beeswax for trade. They lived in small, often temporary settlements, characterized by sunken log-cabins or pit-houses, which provided warmth and shelter in the harsh northern climate. These early communities were organized around kinship and clan structures. By the 8th and 9th centuries, more permanent and fortified settlements, known as *horodyshcha* or *grad*, began to appear on high riverbanks and hilltops, precursors to the medieval towns and cities that would soon arise. It was from these burgeoning centers of political and economic power, established by the Dregovichi, Radimichi, and especially the Krivichi, that the first stirrings of statehood would emerge. The stage was being set for the rise of powerful local principalities, chief among them the Principality of Polotsk, which would come to dominate the lands of Belarus and challenge the growing might of Kyiv.

CHAPTER TWO: The Principality of Polotsk: A Rival to Kyiv

While the burgeoning state of Kievan Rus' sought to consolidate its power along the Dnieper River, another center of East Slavic authority was rising in the north, built on the ambition and fierce independence of the Krivichi. This was the Principality of Polotsk. Strategically located on the banks of the Western Dvina, the city of Polotsk was a vital hub on the great trade artery that linked the Baltic Sea with the Black Sea, the famed "Route from the Varangians to the Greeks." This commanding position gave its rulers immense economic leverage and a distinct worldview, one that often looked westward toward the Baltic and Scandinavia as much as it did south toward Kyiv. From this fortified city, a succession of proud and often rebellious princes would carve out a powerful domain, repeatedly challenging Kyiv's claim to preeminence and forging a separate identity that would lay the political groundwork for a distinct Belarusian nation.

The origins of Polotsk's independent streak are rooted in a dramatic, violent, and deeply personal founding story. The *Primary Chronicle* first mentions the city under the year 862, but its emergence as a political force begins in the late 10th century under a semi-legendary Varangian ruler named Rogvolod. Around 980, as the sons of Sviatoslav of Kyiv battled for supremacy, both Vladimir of Novgorod and Yaropolk of Kyiv sought an alliance with Rogvolod by marrying his daughter, the princess Rogneda. When asked, Rogneda proudly rejected Vladimir, stating she would not marry the "son of a bondswoman," a stinging reference to his mother Malusha's lowly status. Taking this as a profound insult, the enraged Vladimir gathered a large army of Varangians and allied Slavic tribes, marched on Polotsk, and sacked the city. In an act of brutal vengeance, the chronicles record that he raped Rogneda in front of her parents before having Rogvolod and his two sons put to the sword.

Having eliminated his rival and forcibly taken Rogneda as a wife, Vladimir went on to seize Kyiv and become the Grand Prince. The trauma of Polotsk's subjugation, however, was not forgotten. Rogneda bore Vladimir several children, including a son named Izyaslav. Legend holds that Rogneda later attempted to assassinate Vladimir in his sleep, but was stopped at the last moment. When Vladimir prepared to execute her, their young son Izyaslav is said to have rushed to her defense with a sword in his hand. Moved by the boy's courage, and perhaps advised by his boyars, Vladimir relented. He restored the Principality of Polotsk and exiled Rogneda and Izyaslav to rule over her ancestral lands. This act had lasting consequences. Izyaslav and his descendants, the Izyaslavichi, established a separate branch of the Rurikid dynasty. They saw themselves not as appointees of Kyiv, but as the rightful heirs of Rogvolod, nursing a legacy of grievance and a powerful desire for autonomy.

This spirit of defiance was embodied by Izyaslav's son, Bryachislav, who ruled from roughly 1001 to 1044. Bryachislav saw no reason to bow to his powerful uncle in Kyiv, Yaroslav the Wise. Tensions were high because, according to the complex system of Rurikid succession, the descendants of Izyaslav were considered *izgoi*, or "outcast" princes, excluded from the rotation for the grand princely throne in Kyiv because their father had never reigned there. Refusing to accept this subordinate status, Bryachislav went on the offensive. In 1021, he launched a daring raid on the great northern city of Novgorod, a key source of Kyiv's wealth, and sacked it. On his return journey, he was intercepted by Yaroslav's army and defeated at the Sudoma River. Yet, even in defeat, Bryachislav negotiated from a position of strength. The resulting peace treaty forced him to relinquish his Novgorodian plunder, but it also secured Polotsk's control over the strategic towns of Vitebsk and Usvyaty, expanding the principality's territory and cementing its status as a significant regional power.

The golden age of Polotsk's power and independence, however, arrived with Bryachislav's son, Vseslav, a ruler so dynamic, cunning, and seemingly tireless that he became a figure of legend. Reigning for an astonishing 57 years, from 1044 to 1101, Vseslav was known to posterity as *Vseslav the Sorcerer*. The chronicles, likely reflecting folk traditions, claimed he was born with a caul on his head, a sign of supernatural power, and medieval epic poetry like *The Tale of Igor's Campaign* depicted him as a werewolf, capable of racing as a wolf by night from Kyiv to the distant southern outpost of Tmutorokan before the cock crowed. These fantastical tales likely served to explain his uncanny ability to appear suddenly with his armies where he was least expected, a testament to his formidable military and political acumen.

Vseslav's ambition was monumental, and he was determined to elevate Polotsk to a status equal to that of Kyiv and Novgorod. The most potent symbol of this ambition was the construction of the Cathedral of Saint Sophia in Polotsk, built between 1044 and 1066. At the time, only Kyiv and Novgorod possessed cathedrals dedicated to the Holy Wisdom, a clear statement of their supreme political and religious standing. By building his own Saint Sophia, Vseslav was making an audacious claim: Polotsk was their peer. Standing on the high bank of the Western Dvina, it was a powerful piece of political architecture, a declaration in stone and mortar that Polotsk bowed to no one.

Vseslav spent the majority of his long reign in near-constant conflict with the sons of Yaroslav the Wise, the triumvirate of Izyaslav, Sviatoslav, and Vsevolod who jointly ruled Kievan Rus'. He launched raids on their territories, seeking to expand his influence and disrupt their authority. In the winter of 1066–1067, he mounted a particularly audacious campaign, marching on Novgorod once more. This time he not only pillaged the city but also removed the great bell from its Saint Sophia Cathedral to hang in his own, a deeply symbolic act of appropriation and humiliation.

The Yaroslavichi brothers could not let this challenge stand. They united their forces and, in the winter of 1067, marched north into Vseslav's territory, sacking the Polotsk-controlled town of Minsk in the process. On March 3, 1067, the two armies met in a brutal confrontation on the frozen Nemiga River. The battle was a bloodbath, so savage that its memory echoed centuries later in *The

Tale of Igor's Campaign, which described the "bloody banks of the Nemiga" being sown not with grain, but with the bones of the sons of Rus'. Vseslav was defeated, but the victory was costly for the Kyivan princes.

A few months later, the Yaroslavichi invited Vseslav to peace talks near the city of Orsha, swearing a solemn oath on the cross that he would not be harmed. Vseslav accepted their promise, but it was a trap. The brothers violated their oath, seized Vseslav and his two sons, and carted them off to Kyiv, where they were imprisoned in a deep pit. Vseslav's career seemed to be over. But his story took another extraordinary turn the following year, in 1068. After the Kyivan forces suffered a devastating defeat at the hands of the nomadic Polovtsians, the people of Kyiv rose up in rebellion against their own prince, Izyaslav. Storming the prison, the mob freed the charismatic Prince of Polotsk and, in a stunning reversal of fortune, proclaimed Vseslav the Sorcerer as the new Grand Prince of Kyiv.

His reign in the mother of Rus' cities was brief, lasting only seven months. When Izyaslav returned in 1069 with Polish reinforcements, Vseslav, lacking a strong base of support so far from home, fled Kyiv and returned to his native Polotsk. After several more years of struggle, he managed to firmly re-establish his rule there by 1071, where he would remain for the last thirty years of his life, a constant thorn in the side of Kyiv and its rulers, particularly the formidable Vladimir Monomakh.

The power wielded by Vseslav and his predecessors was built on more than just military might. Polotsk's economy thrived due to its control over the Western Dvina trade route, which connected the interior with the rich markets of the Baltic. Merchants exported furs, wax, honey, and slaves, returning with Arab silver dirhams, Byzantine silks, and Scandinavian weaponry. This trade fostered a wealthy and assertive merchant class and a cosmopolitan urban culture. The governance of the principality reflected this. While the Prince (*Knyaz*) and his military retinue (*druzhina*) held executive power, their authority was balanced by a powerful popular assembly known as the *veche*. Composed of the city's free male citizens, the veche in Polotsk was particularly influential and could be a rowdy affair, capable of ratifying treaties, declaring war, and, on occasion, even expelling an unpopular prince.

With the adoption of Orthodox Christianity, Polotsk also became a major religious and cultural center. A bishopric was established, monasteries were founded, and literacy spread, as evidenced by archaeological finds of birch-bark documents. Local artisans developed highly skilled traditions in jewelry making, stone carving, and architecture, creating a distinct Polotskian cultural identity.

The peak of Polotsk's power under Vseslav, however, proved difficult to sustain. Upon his death in 1101, his many sons, in accordance with the established Rurikid practice, divided the vast principality among themselves. This act of inheritance led to the fragmentation of Polotsk's power, as the land was splintered into smaller, feuding appanage principalities centered on cities like Minsk, Vitebsk, and Drutsk. This internal division fatally weakened the state. The princes of Kyiv, particularly Vladimir Monomakh and his son Mstislav the Great, took advantage of the infighting. In the 1120s, Mstislav launched a major campaign against the Polotskian lands, sacking the city and temporarily exiling its ruling family to the distant Byzantine Empire.

Although the principality would later regain a measure of independence, it never fully recovered the unity and strength it had possessed under Vseslav. Internally divided and exhausted by endless conflict with its neighbors, Polotsk became increasingly vulnerable to new external pressures. To the west, the crusading German knights of the Livonian Order were establishing a foothold on the Baltic coast, threatening Polotsk's access to trade. And to the northwest, in the dense forests and marshlands, a new and formidable power was on the rise: the pagan tribes of Lithuania. The long era of Polotsk's dominance was drawing to a close, and the lands of Belarus were about to enter a new and decisive chapter in their history, one defined not by rivalry with Kyiv, but by union with Vilnius.

CHAPTER THREE: The Grand Duchy of Lithuania: A Union of Peoples

The middle of the 13th century was a time of profound crisis for the lands of Rus'. The Mongol invasions had shattered the old political order, leaving a power vacuum in their wake. Kyiv, the mother of Rus' cities, lay in ruins, its authority extinguished. The principalities of Polotsk, Turov, and Minsk, already weakened by internal fragmentation, were left isolated and vulnerable. Into this chaotic landscape stepped a new and formidable force, one that would not only reshape the political map of Eastern Europe but also create a unique state in which the destinies of the Belarusian and Lithuanian peoples would become intertwined for the next five hundred years. This new power was the Grand Duchy of Lithuania.

To their Slavic neighbors, the Lithuanians were a known, if often troublesome, presence. They were a collection of hardy, pagan Baltic tribes who inhabited the dense forests and marshlands to the northwest. For centuries, they had been a source of nuisance raids, but they were now beginning to coalesce into a more organized and dangerous political entity. This unification was not born of grand ambition alone, but of dire necessity. From the west, the crusading Teutonic and Livonian Knights sought to conquer and convert their lands by the sword, while the shadow of the Mongol Golden Horde loomed menacingly in the east. Squeezed between these two implacable foes, the Lithuanian tribes had a stark choice: unite or be annihilated.

The man who rose to this challenge, forging a state from a loose confederation of warrior clans, was Mindaugas. A figure of ruthless pragmatism and strategic genius, Mindaugas consolidated his power through a combination of warfare, strategic marriages, and the occasional murder of his rivals. By the 1240s, he had established himself as the supreme leader of the Lithuanians. Facing immense pressure from the Livonian Order, Mindaugas made a shrewd geopolitical move. In 1251, he agreed to be baptized as a Roman Catholic, and two years later, on July 6, 1253, he was crowned King of Lithuania with the blessing of Pope Innocent IV. This conversion, though likely a matter of political convenience which he would later renounce, temporarily neutralized the threat of the crusaders and granted his nascent state international recognition.

With his western flank momentarily secured, Mindaugas began to expand his domain into the Slavic lands to the southeast, including the region known as Black Ruthenia, centered on the city of Navahrudak. This expansion set a pattern that would define the growth of the Grand Duchy for the next century and a half. It was a process less of outright conquest and more of gradual absorption. The Slavic principalities, leaderless and fearing Mongol raids far more than the rule of a pagan Lithuanian duke, often submitted voluntarily or through negotiated agreements. The local boyars, or nobility, were typically allowed to keep their lands, their Orthodox faith, and a significant degree of autonomy in exchange for pledging allegiance to a new, powerful protector. It was a pragmatic arrangement that offered stability in a world turned upside down.

The resulting state was a remarkable and unique entity. The Grand Duchy of Lithuania, as it came to be known, was a pagan dynasty ruling over a population that was overwhelmingly East Slavic and Orthodox Christian. The Slavic lands were not only more populous but also possessed a more developed culture, a written language, and established systems of law and administration. In a striking reversal of the usual conqueror-conquered dynamic, the Lithuanian ruling class began to adopt the customs and administrative practices of their more sophisticated subjects.

This cultural fusion was most evident in the corridors of power. The official language of the Grand Duchy's chancellery, used for laws, diplomacy, and record-keeping, was not Lithuanian—a language which at the time had no written tradition—but the Ruthenian language, a precursor to modern Belarusian and Ukrainian. This "Old Belarusian," as it is often called in national historiography, became the administrative backbone of the multi-ethnic state. The Lithuanian elite readily adapted the established Slavic models of governance, law, and military organization, creating a synthesis of Baltic and Slavic traditions.

The architects of this expansionist policy were the rulers who followed Mindaugas, particularly those of the Gediminid dynasty, which would come to rule over a vast territory stretching from the Baltic to the Black Sea. Gediminas, who reigned as Grand Duke from about 1316 to 1341, was a master of statecraft. He continued to absorb Slavic lands through a deft mix of military pressure and astute diplomacy, most notably by marrying his many sons and daughters into the ruling families of the surrounding principalities. He established his permanent capital at Vilnius, and in a series of famous letters to the Pope and the cities of the Hanseatic League, he invited knights, merchants, and artisans from across Europe to settle in his realm, promising them tolerance and favorable conditions. Under Gediminas, the principalities of Polotsk (1307), Vitebsk (1320), and Minsk were formally incorporated into the Grand Duchy, bringing the core of the Belarusian lands under a single ruler.

The task of governing this sprawling, diverse state fell to Gediminas's sons, Algirdas and Kęstutis, who ruled jointly from 1345 in a remarkable display of fraternal cooperation. The stoic Kęstutis took charge of the western frontier, dedicating his life to the relentless and exhausting war against the Teutonic Knights. This freed the more ambitious Algirdas to focus on eastward and southward expansion. He styled himself "Grand Duke of the Lithuanians and of the Ruthenians," a title that accurately reflected the dual nature of his state.

Algirdas's reign was marked by a series of brilliant military campaigns that dramatically extended the Duchy's borders. Taking advantage of internal strife within the Golden Horde, he pushed deep into the lands of former Kievan Rus'. His most stunning victory came around 1362 at the Battle of the Blue Waters (on the Syniukha River), where his Lithuanian-Ruthenian army decisively defeated a force of three Mongol commanders. This pivotal, though often overlooked, battle effectively broke the Mongol hold over the region. In the aftermath, Algirdas captured the ancient city of Kyiv, installing his son Vladimir as its prince. By the end of Algirdas's rule in 1377, the Slavic lands of modern-day Belarus and much of Ukraine constituted roughly ninety percent of the Grand Duchy's territory, creating an empire that was geographically the largest state in Europe.

Throughout this period of expansion, a policy of pragmatic religious tolerance generally prevailed. While the ruling dukes and their immediate retinues remained steadfastly pagan, worshiping Perkūnas the thunder god, they understood that governing a vast Christian population required a light touch. Orthodox Christians were largely free to practice their faith, and Orthodox churches and monasteries continued to function. Gediminas had famously declared in his letters that he respected the Christian God, and while Algirdas remained a pagan to his core, he allowed the construction of Orthodox churches in Vilnius for his Ruthenian wives. This tolerance was not an expression of modern liberal values but a practical necessity for maintaining stability in a multiconfessional state. It stood in stark contrast to the religious uniformity demanded by a crusading Catholic Europe and the rising Orthodox power of Muscovy.

The Grand Duchy of Lithuania was, in essence, a federation. The local Slavic nobility retained their privileges, their faith, and their influence in local affairs, bound by an oath of loyalty to the Grand Duke in Vilnius. This decentralized structure allowed for the rapid and relatively peaceful integration of vast territories. For the nobility of the Belarusian lands, this new arrangement was far from a foreign occupation. It was a partnership that provided security from external threats and preserved their traditional way of life. They were becoming integral members of a new political community, one that was Lithuanian by dynasty but predominantly Slavic in language, culture, and population.

However, the immense state built by Mindaugas, Gediminas, and Algirdas faced growing external pressures. The war with the Teutonic Knights remained a fight for survival, a bloody, grinding conflict that drained the state's resources. In the east, the

Principality of Moscow was beginning to consolidate its power, presenting itself as the rightful heir to Kievan Rus' and the sole defender of the Orthodox faith. Caught between these two formidable powers, Algirdas's son and successor, Jogaila, faced a momentous decision that would set the course for the next four centuries. The era of pagan Lithuania was drawing to a close, and the question of its future—whether it would align with the Catholic West or the Orthodox East—had to be answered.

CHAPTER FOUR: The Golden Age: Culture and Law in the Grand Duchy

The period stretching from the late fourteenth to the mid-sixteenth century marked a distinct flourishing of culture, law, and society within the Ruthenian lands of the Grand Duchy of Lithuania. Having secured its vast borders and established a unique political system, the Duchy entered an era of relative stability that allowed for profound internal development. This was not an age of ethnic Belarusian nationalism in the modern sense, but it was a time when the language, laws, and traditions of the region's East Slavic inhabitants formed the very bedrock of a powerful, multi-ethnic state. From the sophisticated legal codes drafted in the state chancellery to the defiant stone walls of fortified Orthodox churches, the Belarusian lands forged a unique identity, blending the heritage of Rus' with the dynamism of Renaissance Europe.

At the heart of this "Golden Age" was the development of one of Europe's most advanced legal systems, codified in the Statutes of Lithuania. These were not mere collections of old customs but comprehensive legal codes that governed everything from property rights to criminal procedure. Critically, they were written not in Latin or Lithuanian, but in the Ruthenian language, the East Slavic tongue that served as the official language of the state. This Chancery Slavonic, a predecessor to modern Belarusian and Ukrainian, was the language of administration and justice, ensuring that the legal and cultural norms of the majority population were enshrined at the highest level. The creation of the Statutes was a monumental undertaking, reflecting a society that valued order, precedent, and the rule of law.

The first of these great legal compilations, the Statute of 1529, was a landmark achievement initiated by the Grand Duchy's Council of Lords and approved by Grand Duke Sigismund I. It consisted of 13 chapters and 282 articles, drawing on sources as diverse as old Rus' law, local customs, and international treaties. For the first time, it systematically organized the laws of the land, establishing a clear framework for governance and the rights of the nobility. This was followed by the Second Statute in 1566, a more advanced code that expanded upon its predecessor and, significantly, made the legal rights of Orthodox and Catholic nobles equal. The pressure for this revision came from the nobility itself, a testament to the growing power and political consciousness of this elite class.

The final and most famous of the three was the Third Statute of 1588, championed by the great statesman and chancellor Lew Sapieha. This was the pinnacle of the Grand Duchy's legal tradition, a sophisticated code that separated the powers of the monarch, the parliament (*Seimas*), and the courts, a principle remarkably advanced for its time. The Third Statute remained the law of the land for over 250 years, even after the Grand Duchy was absorbed by the Russian Empire, and was only abolished in 1840. Its influence was immense, shaping the legal codes of neighboring lands, including Muscovy's *Sobornoye Ulozheniye* of 1649. More than just a law book, the Statutes were a powerful declaration of the Grand Duchy's sovereignty and distinct legal identity, particularly in its relationship with the Kingdom of Poland.

This cultural confidence was embodied by the remarkable figure of Francysk Skaryna, a true Renaissance man from the city of Polotsk. A scholar, doctor, publisher, and translator, Skaryna's life work was driven by a humanist desire to make knowledge accessible to the common people. After studying at universities in Kraków and Padua, where he earned a doctorate in medicine, he set his sights on a revolutionary goal: printing the Bible in a language his people could understand. Setting up a press in Prague, he published his first book, the Psalter, on August 6, 1517. This was the first printed book in any East Slavic language.

Between 1517 and 1519, Skaryna translated and printed 23 books of the Old Testament. His edition, titled the *Bibliya Ruska* ("Ruthenian Bible"), was a monumental achievement. The language he used was a Belarusian recension of Church Slavonic, enriched with vernacular elements to make it more comprehensible to a lay audience. Crucially, Skaryna included his own prefaces and commentaries, in which he explained the texts and promoted ideals of education and humanism, encouraging readers to reflect on what they read. His work predated many other vernacular translations of the Bible in Europe and laid the foundation for the modern Belarusian literary language. Though an attempt to distribute his books in Moscow was rebuffed, they circulated widely throughout the Grand Duchy, profoundly influencing the region's spiritual and cultural life for generations.

The creative energy of the era also found expression in stone and brick. A distinctive architectural style known as Belarusian Gothic emerged, blending traditional Byzantine Orthodox designs with the soaring verticality and defensive features of Western European Gothic. This style was particularly evident in the construction of fortified churches, buildings that had to serve not only as houses of worship but also as sanctuaries in a land frequently threatened by invasion.

Prime examples of this unique style can still be seen in the Church of St. Michael in Synkavichy and the Church of the Nativity of the Blessed Virgin Mary in Muravanka. These structures are characterized by thick, one-and-a-half-meter walls, high-set windows, and four imposing defensive towers at the corners, giving them the appearance of small castles. Inside, however, Gothic elements like ribbed vaults and pointed arches created spaces of grace and height. This architectural fusion was a physical manifestation of the Grand Duchy's character: a state culturally rooted in the Orthodox East but open to the influences of the Catholic West. Castles, too, were built in this period, with the foundations of future magnate strongholds like Mir Castle being laid.

Society in the Grand Duchy was rigidly hierarchical. At the apex were the great magnate families—names like Radziwiłł, Sapieha, and Ostrogski—who controlled vast estates and wielded immense political power. Below them was the broader nobility, the *szlachta*. This class, comprising both ethnically Lithuanian and Ruthenian families, began to merge into a single, legally privileged estate.

Originally a warrior class of boyars, their rights and freedoms were increasingly codified by the Statutes of Lithuania, solidifying their position as the dominant political force in the state. The *szlachta* constituted a remarkably high percentage of the population, perhaps as much as 10 percent, far greater than in most other European countries.

Below the nobility were the townspeople, or burghers, who benefited from the growth of urban centers like Polotsk, Vitebsk, Navahrudak, and Minsk. Many of these cities were granted Magdeburg Law, a German legal code that gave them a significant degree of self-government. First granted to Brest in 1390, and later to cities like Polotsk (1498) and Minsk (1499), this right allowed towns to have their own councils (*magistrates*), courts, and economic privileges. This autonomy fostered a vibrant urban culture of merchants and artisans, who thrived on the trade routes that crisscrossed the duchy, connecting the Baltic and Black Seas. The bulk of the population, however, consisted of peasants, many of whom were being gradually enserfed, their labor tied to the estates of the nobility and the church.

For much of this period, a pragmatic policy of religious tolerance prevailed. Although the ruling Jagiellonian dynasty had converted to Roman Catholicism in 1386 to secure the Polish crown, the vast majority of their Ruthenian subjects remained Orthodox. The state understood that stability depended on respecting the faith of the population. Orthodox nobles enjoyed the same legal rights as their Catholic counterparts, and the Ruthenian language of the Orthodox majority was the language of the state itself. This multicultural and multiconfessional reality was a defining feature of the Grand Duchy, setting it apart from the more religiously uniform states of Western Europe and the increasingly centralized Orthodox state of Muscovy. This delicate balance, however, was about to be tested by the seismic forces of the Reformation and Counter-Reformation, and by a deepening political union with Poland that would forge a new reality for the people of the Belarusian lands.

CHAPTER FIVE: The Polish-Lithuanian Commonwealth: A New Political Reality

The relationship that bound the Grand Duchy of Lithuania and the Kingdom of Poland was a centuries-long courtship, marked by moments of passionate alliance, tense negotiation, and a persistent reluctance to fully commit. It was a union born not of romantic sentiment, but of cold, hard geopolitical necessity. For the Belarusian lands, this evolving partnership would fundamentally alter their political, cultural, and religious trajectory, drawing them ever deeper into the orbit of the West and creating a new state of unprecedented scale and complexity in Eastern Europe.

The first serious marriage proposal came in 1385 with the Union of Krewo. The deal was straightforward: Jogaila, the pagan Grand Duke of Lithuania, would marry the young Queen Jadwiga of Poland. In return, he and his Lithuanian subjects would convert to Roman Catholicism, and he would become King of Poland. The primary motivation was mutual survival. Both states faced the relentless aggression of the Teutonic Knights, a crusading military order that used Lithuania's paganism as a perpetual justification for invasion. By converting, Jogaila removed the Knights' primary excuse for war and gained a powerful ally. For the Polish nobles, the union brought a vast eastern realm under their new king's authority, neutralizing a potential rival and securing their own frontiers.

The terms of the agreement, signed at Kreva Castle in what is now Belarus, were deliberately vague on a crucial point. The Latin text stated that Jogaila promised to *applicare*, or "attach," his Lithuanian and Ruthenian lands to the Polish Crown. What "attach" actually meant would be debated for the next two centuries. Polish lords interpreted it as a full incorporation of the Grand Duchy into their kingdom. The Lithuanian and Ruthenian nobility, however, saw it as an alliance of two sovereign states, a partnership of equals. This fundamental disagreement set the stage for a long-running political drama.

The most forceful advocate for the Grand Duchy's independence was Jogaila's cousin, Vytautas. A brilliant and restless military commander, Vytautas was not content to be a mere governor for a king in Kraków. He engaged in a complex series of political maneuvers, at times even allying with his old enemies, the Teutonic Knights, to assert his authority. His persistence paid off. The Union of Vilnius and Radom in 1401 formally recognized Vytautas as the Grand Duke of Lithuania, with full authority for his lifetime, though acknowledging Jogaila (now known in Poland as Władysław II Jagiełło) as his overlord.

The wisdom of this uneasy alliance was demonstrated spectacularly on the fields of Grunwald on July 15, 1410. A massive combined army of Poles and Lithuanians, which included three banners of troops from Smolensk, confronted the might of the Teutonic Order. The battle was one of the largest in medieval Europe, a brutal clash of heavy cavalry and infantry. After a day of ferocious fighting, the Polish-Lithuanian forces achieved a crushing victory, killing or capturing most of the Teutonic leadership. Though the allies failed to take the Knights' capital at Malbork, the Order's military power was broken forever. The victory at Grunwald cemented the Polish-Lithuanian union as the dominant force in the region and became a foundational myth for the nations involved.

For the next century and a half, the two states were governed under this system of personal union, linked by the Jagiellonian dynasty descended from Jogaila. The Grand Duchy of Lithuania fiercely guarded its autonomy, maintaining its own laws, army, and administration. The Ruthenian nobility of the Belarusian lands continued to thrive, their language serving as the official tongue of the state. However, the external pressures that had first brought the two powers together did not disappear; they simply changed direction.

By the mid-16th century, a new and more formidable threat was rising in the east. The Grand Duchy of Moscow, now styling itself as the Tsardom of Russia under the formidable Ivan IV, "the Terrible," was determined to expand westward. Ivan's primary goal was to gain access to the Baltic Sea, a prize currently controlled by the Livonian Confederation, a weak collection of German-led territories in modern-day Latvia and Estonia. In 1558, Ivan invaded, launching the long and bloody Livonian War. The Livonian Order, unable to fend off the Russian armies, collapsed and sought protection from its neighbors. The Grand Duchy of Lithuania was drawn into the conflict, and soon found itself bearing the brunt of a full-scale Russian invasion.

The war proved disastrous for Lithuania. Russian armies captured the strategic city of Polotsk in 1563, a devastating blow both militarily and psychologically. The Grand Duchy's resources were stretched to the breaking point. It became clear to many that Lithuania could not win this war alone. The Polish Crown, however, was reluctant to commit fully to a conflict that primarily concerned its neighbor. This crisis brought the question of the union to a head. A deeper, more permanent bond was no longer a theoretical debate; it was a matter of survival.

The push for a tighter union also came from within the Grand Duchy. The middle and lower *szlachta* (nobility) looked with envy at their Polish counterparts, who enjoyed extensive legal and political privileges known as the "Golden Liberty." This system gave the Polish nobility the right to elect their king, significant power in their parliament (the *Sejm*), and broad protections against monarchical overreach. The Ruthenian and Lithuanian nobles desired these same freedoms and saw a full union with Poland as the surest way to secure them. The powerful magnates of the Grand Duchy, however, were deeply opposed, fearing that a merger would dilute their immense power and wealth.

The final impetus came from a biological reality: King Sigismund II Augustus, ruler of both states, was childless. With the Jagiellonian dynasty on the verge of extinction, there was a real danger that upon his death, Poland and Lithuania would elect separate rulers and the union would dissolve entirely, leaving Lithuania to face Moscow alone.

In 1569, Sigismund II Augustus summoned a joint Sejm to the city of Lublin to forge a permanent settlement. The negotiations were fraught with tension. The Lithuanian magnates, led by Mikołaj "the Red" Radziwiłł, put up stiff resistance, arguing fiercely to preserve the Grand Duchy's sovereignty. When the talks stalled, they packed their bags and left Lublin in protest. In response, the King made a dramatic and ruthless move. He issued an edict unilaterally annexing the southern provinces of the Grand Duchy—Podlachia, Volhynia, Bracław, and Kyiv—directly into the Kingdom of Poland. These lands, comprising much of modern Ukraine, were home to many of the Ruthenian nobles who had been clamoring for union.

This act broke the back of the Lithuanian resistance. Faced with the dismemberment of their state, the magnates had no choice but to return to the negotiating table. On July 1, 1569, the Union of Lublin was formally agreed upon, creating a new political entity: the Polish-Lithuanian Commonwealth, or the *Rzeczpospolita Obojga Narodów* (Republic of Both Nations).

The Commonwealth was a unique creation in 16th-century Europe. It was a federal state, a republic in name, and an elective monarchy in practice. Poland and Lithuania were to be a single, indivisible body politic with a jointly elected king who would be both King of Poland and Grand Duke of Lithuania. They would share a common parliament, a single foreign policy, and a unified currency.

Crucially, however, the Grand Duchy of Lithuania retained a significant degree of autonomy. It kept its own name, territory, administration, treasury, and army. Most importantly, it kept its own legal system, based on the Statutes of Lithuania. In a powerful assertion of its continued legal separateness, the Third Statute of Lithuania was formally adopted in 1588, nearly two decades *after* the Union of Lublin. This landmark legal code explicitly stated that the Commonwealth was a federation of two equal states and included provisions to protect the Grand Duchy's interests.

For the Belarusian lands, which now formed the core of the Grand Duchy after the detachment of the Ukrainian provinces, the new reality was complex. The Ruthenian nobility fully entered the world of the Polish *szlachta*. They gained the coveted "Golden Liberties," participating in the rowdy royal elections and sending deputies to the common Sejm in Warsaw. This political integration accelerated a process of cultural Polonization. The Polish language, already fashionable, increasingly became the language of high culture and politics among the upper classes. Many noble families, initially Orthodox and Ruthenian-speaking, began to adopt Polish customs and, over time, the Catholic faith. This shift created a growing cultural gap between the Polonized nobility and the Ruthenian-speaking Orthodox peasantry. The common saying, *gente Ruthenus, natione Polonus* ("of Ruthenian stock, of the Polish nation"), came to define this new identity, where cultural allegiance to Poland coexisted with a regional origin. The new political reality had brought security and new freedoms for the elite, but it also set in motion profound cultural and religious transformations that would define the next two centuries.

CHAPTER SIX: Religious Strife and the Rise of the Uniate Church

For a time, the Polish-Lithuanian Commonwealth enjoyed a reputation as a "state without stakes," a rare haven of relative religious tolerance in a 16th-century Europe consumed by brutal wars of faith. The Warsaw Confederation of 1573 had legally guaranteed freedom of religion for the nobility, creating a society where Catholics, Orthodox Christians, a growing variety of Protestants, and even Jews and Muslims could coexist with a degree of peace unknown in the lands of the St. Bartholomew's Day Massacre or the Spanish Inquisition. This pluralism, however, was not the product of a deeply held philosophical commitment to diversity; it was a pragmatic necessity in a vast, multi-ethnic state. As the century drew to a close, this delicate balance came under immense strain from two powerful and competing religious movements: the Protestant Reformation and the Catholic Counter-Reformation. Caught in the middle, the Orthodox Church of the Belarusian lands would be fractured by a dramatic and divisive attempt at union with Rome.

The ideas of the Reformation arrived early in the Grand Duchy of Lithuania, finding particularly fertile ground among the powerful magnate families. For men like Mikołaj "the Black" Radziwiłł, the Palatine of Vilnius and Grand Chancellor of Lithuania, Calvinism was more than a spiritual awakening. It was a potent political tool. By embracing Protestantism, the magnates could assert their independence from the Catholic-dominated Polish crown, seize church lands and revenues, and establish a faith that emphasized the authority of secular rulers over a distant papacy. Radziwiłł became a zealous patron of the new faith, funding the translation and printing of the first Protestant Bible in Polish at Brest in 1563. For a time, it seemed the Reformation might triumph among the elite; by the 1580s, a majority of the senators from the Grand Duchy were Calvinist or another Protestant denomination.

This Protestant ascendancy, however, provoked a vigorous and highly effective response from the Catholic Church. The Counter-Reformation was not primarily a campaign of fire and sword in the Commonwealth, but one of intellect, education, and persuasion. Its vanguard was the Society of Jesus, the Jesuits, who were invited into the realm in 1564. Spearheaded by brilliant polemicists like Piotr Skarga, the Jesuits focused their efforts on winning back the hearts and minds of the nobility. They established a network of elite schools and colleges, most notably the academy in Vilnius, which would become Vilnius University in 1579. These institutions offered a superb humanist education that soon surpassed anything the Protestant schools could offer, attracting the sons of the nobility regardless of their faith. Through sophisticated preaching, intellectual debate, and shrewd political maneuvering at court, the Jesuits successfully engineered a mass reconversion of the magnate families back to Catholicism over the next few generations.

Caught between the intellectual appeal of Protestantism and the resurgent power of Catholicism was the Ruthenian Orthodox Church, the traditional faith of the Belarusian and Ukrainian populations. The Orthodox Church found itself in a precarious position. For centuries, it had been under the jurisdiction of the Patriarch of Constantinople, but after the fall of that city to the Ottoman Turks, the patriarch was a subjugated figure, unable to provide effective leadership. The situation was complicated further in 1589 when Patriarch Jeremias II, traveling through the region, elevated the status of the church in Moscow to a patriarchate, creating a powerful new rival religious center to the east. Within the Commonwealth, the Orthodox hierarchy faced numerous challenges. The Polish king, a Catholic, often appointed bishops based on political loyalty rather than spiritual fitness. The church was losing its most powerful patrons, the Ruthenian magnates, who were converting to Calvinism and, later, back to Catholicism. Furthermore, a system of powerful lay brotherhoods had emerged, particularly in cities like Vilnius and Lviv, which challenged the authority of the bishops and sought to reform the church from below.

It was in this climate of crisis and vulnerability that a group of Orthodox bishops conceived a radical solution: a union with the Church of Rome. The idea was not entirely new, having been attempted at the Council of Florence in 1439, but now it gained a new urgency. Led by bishops such as Ipatii Potii of Volodymyr and Kyrylo Terletskyi of Lutsk, the proponents of union had several motivations. They sought to escape the decaying authority of Constantinople and the perceived threat of the new Moscow Patriarchate. They also desperately wanted to elevate their own status; as Orthodox bishops, they had no seats in the Commonwealth's Senate, unlike their Roman Catholic counterparts. A union with Rome, they believed, would grant them political equality, strengthen their authority over the laity and lower clergy, and provide the institutional support needed to reform their church and combat the influence of the Protestants.

The project found a powerful ally in King Sigismund III Vasa, a devout Catholic and product of a Jesuit education, who saw the union as a way to religiously unify his kingdom and sever his Orthodox subjects' ties to foreign powers. After secret negotiations, Bishops Potii and Terletskyi traveled to Rome. In December 1595, in a grand ceremony in the Vatican, they formally declared their acceptance of papal authority and Catholic doctrine on behalf of the Ruthenian episcopate. Pope Clement VIII, in turn, issued bulls guaranteeing that the Ruthenian church could retain its ancient Byzantine rite, its use of the Church Slavonic language, and its distinct customs, such as a married priesthood.

The final act was to take place in October 1596, when a synod was convened in the city of Brest to formally proclaim the union. From the very beginning, the proceedings were fraught with division. The unionists, led by Metropolitan Michael Rohoza and a majority of the bishops, met in one location. But a large and powerful opposition faction, which included two of the bishops, influential clergy, representatives of the lay brotherhoods, and, most importantly, the wealthiest and most powerful Orthodox magnate in the Commonwealth, Prince Konstanty Ostrogski, held a rival anti-union synod in the same city. Ostrogski, who had initially been open to the idea of a universal church union, had turned against this specific plan, viewing it as a secret conspiracy by a handful of bishops that betrayed the Orthodox faith without proper consultation with the wider church or the eastern patriarchs.

The result was not unity, but a schism that tore the Ruthenian church and people apart. The pro-union synod proclaimed the creation of the Ruthenian Uniate Church (later known as the Greek Catholic Church), which was immediately recognized by the king and the pope as the sole legitimate Eastern church in the Commonwealth. The anti-union synod, in turn, excommunicated the unionist bishops and declared its continued loyalty to the Orthodox faith. The state threw its full weight behind the new Uniate Church. Orthodoxy was now officially illegal. A bitter struggle began for control of churches, monasteries, and land, a conflict described by contemporaries as "Rus' fighting against Rus'."

The decades that followed were marked by religious strife and persecution. Orthodox believers who refused to accept the union were often violently suppressed, their churches seized and handed over to the Uniates. This coercion was particularly intense in the Belarusian lands. One of the most zealous and effective promoters of the new church was Josaphat Kuntsevych, the Uniate Archbishop of Polotsk. Known to his opponents as the "Soul-Snatcher," Kuntsevych was a devout and ascetic figure who worked tirelessly to enforce the union in his archdiocese. His methods, however, generated immense hostility among the Orthodox townspeople and clergy. The conflict reached a bloody climax on November 12, 1623, when an angry mob in Vitebsk, enraged by his actions, attacked and murdered him, throwing his body into the Dvina river. The state responded with brutal reprisals, executing nearly a hundred citizens and stripping the city of many of its rights. For the Catholic world, Kuntsevych became a martyr and a saint; for the Orthodox, his name became a symbol of oppression.

Despite the state's support, the Uniate Church failed to completely absorb the Orthodox population. The Orthodox Church survived, albeit as a persecuted and underground organization for a time, before regaining official recognition in 1632. It retained the fierce loyalty of many nobles, the urban brotherhoods, and, most critically, the Cossacks in the Ukrainian lands to the south. The Union of Brest had created a new and lasting religious division within the East Slavic people of the Commonwealth. In the Belarusian lands, the Uniate Church would, over the next two centuries, become the faith of the vast majority of the peasantry, creating a religious identity distinct from both the Catholic Polish nobility and the Orthodox Russians. This deep religious fracture, born from a desperate attempt at unity, would have profound consequences, adding a volatile new element to the growing tensions that were beginning to pull the Commonwealth apart.

CHAPTER SEVEN: The Deluge: War with Muscovy and the Decline of the Commonwealth

The middle of the seventeenth century was a time of cataclysm. For the Polish-Lithuanian Commonwealth, and particularly for the Belarusian lands at the core of the Grand Duchy of Lithuania, the period was so ruinous, so utterly devastating, that it would be forever seared into the collective memory as "The Deluge." It was not a single war but a cascade of interlocking conflicts—a Cossack rebellion, a Muscovite invasion, and a Swedish onslaught—that washed away the foundations of the state, leaving behind a landscape of ruin and a permanently altered balance of power in Eastern Europe. The Golden Age of culture and law was consumed by an age of fire and sword, from which the Commonwealth would never fully recover.

The first crack in the dam appeared not in Lithuania, but far to the south, in the vast Ukrainian steppes. In 1648, a charismatic Cossack hetman named Bohdan Khmelnytsky, nursing a potent mix of personal grievances and popular discontent, ignited a massive rebellion. The uprising was fueled by years of simmering resentment among the Orthodox Ruthenian population against the social, political, and religious domination of the Catholic Polish and Polonized magnates. Khmelnytsky's call to arms resonated powerfully with Orthodox peasants, townspeople, and clergy who felt their faith and way of life were under constant threat. Allied with the formidable cavalry of the Crimean Tatars, his Cossack forces inflicted a series of humiliating defeats on the Crown armies in 1648.

The news of these victories spread like wildfire, transforming the Cossack revolt into a widespread social and religious war. The violence was ferocious, with rebels targeting Polish nobles, Catholic and Uniate clergy, and Jewish estate managers, who were often seen as agents of the magnates' authority. Reprisals from the

Commonwealth, led by ruthless commanders like Prince Jeremi Wiśniowiecki, were equally brutal. Though centered in Ukraine, the shockwaves of the uprising were felt immediately in the southern regions of Belarus, where Cossack detachments conducted raids and stirred up local peasant revolts, particularly in the regions of Gomel, Pinsk, and Mozyr. The Commonwealth's eastern frontier was beginning to disintegrate.

For six years, the war in the south raged, bleeding the Commonwealth's armies and treasury dry. Seeing his own forces depleted and his Tatar allies proving unreliable, Khmelnytsky sought a more powerful protector. He found one in Tsar Alexis of Muscovy, who saw a golden opportunity to achieve a long-held Russian ambition: to reclaim the lands of former Kievan Rus' lost to Lithuania centuries earlier and to position himself as the defender of the Orthodox faith. In January 1654, at the Council of Pereiaslav, Khmelnytsky and the Cossack leadership swore an oath of allegiance to the Tsar, effectively placing their nascent state under Moscow's authority. This act transformed the internal rebellion into a full-scale interstate war.

In the summer of 1654, the storm broke over the Grand Duchy of Lithuania. A massive Muscovite army, numbering some 41,000 soldiers nominally led by the Tsar himself, poured across the border. The invasion was justified as a holy war to liberate the Orthodox population from "Latin" and "Uniate" oppression, a message that found some sympathy among the common people in the eastern territories. The Commonwealth was caught completely off guard. Its best forces were still tied down in Ukraine, and the Grand Duchy's army under the command of Grand Hetman Janusz Radziwiłł was woefully outnumbered.

The Muscovite advance was swift and brutal. The border fortresses of Bely and Dorogobuzh fell quickly. Radziwiłł, despite a tactical victory at Shklov, was overwhelmed at the Battle of Shepeleviche and forced into a desperate retreat. One by one, the cities of the Belarusian lands were besieged and captured. Polotsk, the ancient seat of Belarusian statehood, fell, as did Vitebsk and Mogilev. After a three-month siege, the great fortress city of Smolensk, the "key to the Commonwealth," surrendered to the Tsar in October 1654. The road into the heart of the Grand Duchy now lay wide open.

The following year, 1655, brought the apocalypse. As a Lithuanian counter-offensive faltered, the Tsar ordered a new, even larger invasion. The remaining Lithuanian forces offered little resistance. On July 3, Minsk was taken. Then, on August 8, for the first time in its history, the capital of the Grand Duchy, Vilnius, fell to a foreign army. What followed was a three-day massacre and fire that left the city ravaged. Thousands of its citizens were slaughtered, and the city that had been a vibrant center of Renaissance culture was reduced to ruins. The Muscovite forces pressed on, taking Grodno and Kaunas in their wake.

The war was conducted with unparalleled savagery. This was not a conflict of professional armies adhering to chivalric codes; it was a war of annihilation. Cities that resisted were often put to the sword. Entire regions were depopulated as Muscovite forces forcibly relocated tens of thousands of artisans and townspeople deep into Russia to populate its own cities. Famine and plague followed in the wake of the armies, compounding the misery. The toll on the Belarusian lands was catastrophic. It is estimated that in the course of the thirteen-year war, the Grand Duchy of Lithuania lost over half of its population, a demographic blow more severe than that suffered in the Second World War. Towns and villages lay in ashes, the economy was shattered, and the social fabric was torn to shreds.

As the Commonwealth reeled from the Muscovite onslaught in the east, a second predator struck from the north. Seeing the state on the verge of collapse, King Charles X Gustav of Sweden invaded in July 1655, seeking to turn the Baltic Sea into a "Swedish lake." Polish armies melted away, nobles switched their allegiance, and King John II Casimir Vasa was forced to flee the country. The Commonwealth, as a functioning state, effectively ceased to exist.

Faced with this hopeless situation, a faction of the Lithuanian leadership made a radical choice. Grand Hetman Janusz Radziwiłł, the commander of Lithuania's armies, concluded that the union with a collapsing Poland was a dead letter and that salvation lay in an alliance with Stockholm. Accusing the Poles of failing to aid the Grand Duchy in its hour of need, he entered into negotiations with the Swedes. On October 20, 1655, Radziwiłł and his cousin Bogusław signed the Union of Kėdainiai, an act that broke the 186-year-old Union of Lublin. It severed all ties with Poland and placed the Grand Duchy of Lithuania under the protection of the Swedish king, whom they recognized as their new Grand Duke. For Radziwiłł, it was a desperate gamble to save his homeland from Muscovite annihilation; for his opponents, including the powerful Sapieha family, it was an act of high treason.

The Swedish protectorate proved to be no salvation. The Swedish occupation was as brutal and extractive as the Muscovite one, alienating what little support it had. Meanwhile, the sheer ferocity of the foreign invasions began to spark a popular resistance movement in Poland, famously galvanized by the heroic defense of the Jasna Góra monastery. Slowly, improbably, the Commonwealth began to fight back. Alliances shifted as Muscovy, growing wary of Swedish expansion, signed a temporary truce with the Commonwealth in 1656 to fight their mutual rival.

The war dragged on for years, a bloody and exhausting struggle fought across a ravaged landscape. Lithuanian forces loyal to the Commonwealth, led by Paweł Jan Sapieha, waged a civil war against the Radziwiłłs and their Swedish allies, while also battling the Muscovite occupiers. By 1660, the Commonwealth managed to conclude the war with Sweden with the Treaty of Oliva, which largely restored the pre-war border but confirmed Sweden's control over most of Livonia. This allowed King John II Casimir to focus all his remaining strength on the eastern front.

The war with Muscovy ground on for another seven grueling years. The tide began to turn in 1660 when a combined Polish-Lithuanian army defeated a Muscovite force at the Battle of Polonka, near Slonim. Yet neither side could achieve a decisive victory. The Commonwealth was financially ruined and wracked by internal strife, while Muscovy was also exhausted by the long conflict.

Finally, on January 30, 1667, the belligerents signed the Truce of Andrusovo, ending thirteen years of bloodshed. The terms were a disaster for the Commonwealth and a triumph for Muscovy. The Grand Duchy of Lithuania was forced to cede the fortress of Smolensk and all the lands east of the Dnieper River, including Left-Bank Ukraine. Kyiv, the ancient mother of Rus' cities, was handed over to Russia, initially for a two-year period that would become permanent.

The Deluge was over, but it had carved a permanent scar across the face of the region. The demographic and economic destruction was immense. The Grand Duchy of Lithuania was territorially truncated and psychologically broken. The war marked a fundamental shift in the European balance of power, ending the Commonwealth's status as a great power and heralding the inexorable rise of the Tsardom of Russia. The dream of a powerful, multi-ethnic republic stretching from the Baltic to the Black Sea was shattered, its decline now seemingly irreversible.

CHAPTER EIGHT: The Partitions: The End of the Commonwealth and Russian Rule

The century following the horrors of the Deluge was not a period of recovery for the Polish-Lithuanian Commonwealth, but one of long, agonizing decay. The state that emerged from the mid-17th-century wars was a shadow of its former self, an exhausted giant whose immense size belied a fatal internal sickness. While its neighbors—the rising powers of Russia, Prussia, and Austria—were busy building centralized states, modernizing their armies, and embracing the tenets of enlightened absolutism, the Commonwealth slid deeper into a state of political paralysis. For the Belarusian lands of the Grand Duchy of Lithuania, this was an era of stagnation and vulnerability, culminating in the complete erasure of their state from the map of Europe.

The source of this paralysis lay in the very heart of the Commonwealth's political system: the "Golden Liberty" of the nobility. This once-celebrated body of rights had degenerated into a recipe for anarchy. Its most corrosive element was the *liberum veto*, a parliamentary device that allowed any single deputy in the Sejm to nullify all legislation passed during a session and force its immediate dissolution. Born from the principle of unanimity among equals, it became a tool for obstruction, easily exploited by powerful magnates or, increasingly, by foreign ambassadors who could bribe a single deputy to torpedo any reform that threatened their interests. Between 1573 and 1763, roughly a third of all parliamentary sessions were dissolved without passing any legislation, effectively rendering the state ungovernable.

Within the Grand Duchy of Lithuania, this dysfunction allowed powerful magnate families to act as uncrowned kings, maintaining private armies and pursuing their own foreign policies. Feuds between powerful clans, such as the Sapiehas and the Radziwiłłs, could plunge entire regions into private wars, further undermining the authority of the central government. Foreign courts happily poured money into these rivalries, ensuring the Commonwealth remained weak, divided, and pliable.

This weakness was brutally exposed at the dawn of the 18th century, when the Commonwealth became the primary battlefield for the Great Northern War (1700-1721). The conflict pitted a rising Russia under Tsar Peter the Great against the Swedish Empire of the young warrior-king Charles XII. Although the Commonwealth was officially neutral for much of the war, its king, Augustus II the Strong, entered the conflict as the Elector of Saxony. As a result, the Belarusian lands were once again subjected to the misery of marching armies. Swedish, Russian, and Saxon forces crisscrossed the territory, living off the land, requisitioning supplies, and spreading destruction. Charles XII won his last major victory near Golovchin in July 1708, but a few months later, Peter the Great annihilated a crucial Swedish supply corps at the Battle of Lesnaya in the Mogilev region—a victory Peter called "the mother of the victory of Poltava." For the local population, it was another deluge of violence and economic ruin.

The war's outcome sealed the Commonwealth's fate. With Sweden defeated, Russia emerged as the undisputed dominant power in Eastern Europe. Peter the Great now positioned himself as the ultimate arbiter of Commonwealth politics. This new reality was formalized at the infamous "Silent Sejm" of 1717. Summoned to end a civil war between King Augustus II and a confederation of nobles, the session was held under the menacing watch of Russian troops. To prevent the use of the *liberum veto*, only the marshal of the Sejm was permitted to speak. In a single day, the Sejm ratified a treaty that drastically limited the size of the Commonwealth's army to a paltry 24,000 men (only 6,000 for Lithuania) and placed its political system under the formal "guarantee" of the Russian Tsar. The Commonwealth was now, in all but name, a Russian protectorate, its independence effectively terminated.

The subsequent decades under the rule of two Saxon kings, Augustus II and his son Augustus III, were a period of deep stagnation. Yet, by the mid-18th century, the ideas of the Enlightenment began to penetrate the apathy. A powerful reform movement, led by influential families like the Czartoryskis, emerged with the goal of saving the state from collapse. Their chance seemed to come in 1764 with the election of Stanisław August Poniatowski, a sophisticated and reform-minded nobleman, as the last king of the Commonwealth. Poniatowski's election, however, was a paradox; he was placed on the throne by his former lover, the Russian Empress Catherine the Great, who expected him to be a pliant puppet.

When Poniatowski and the reformers began to push for strengthening the state, Catherine grew alarmed. She found a convenient pretext to intervene in the issue of "dissenters"—the rights of Orthodox and Protestant nobles. Acting as their protector, she backed a confederation of conservative, anti-reform nobles. This led to a bloody civil war known as the Confederation of Bar (1768-1772), a chaotic struggle that combined a defense of traditional liberties and Catholicism with an anti-Russian insurrection. After years of fighting, Russian forces crushed the confederation. Citing the Commonwealth's incurable anarchy, Russia, Prussia, and Austria decided to "restore order" by helping themselves to its territory.

On August 5, 1772, the three powers signed a treaty for the First Partition. The Grand Duchy of Lithuania lost a significant portion of its northeastern territory. Russia annexed the lands of what is now eastern Belarus, including the cities of Polotsk, Vitebsk, and Mogilev. Austria seized Galicia in the south, while Prussia took a strategically vital piece of northern Poland. In a single stroke, the Commonwealth lost about 30 percent of its territory and half its population. The truncated state was then forced to ratify this act of dismemberment at a Sejm held under the threat of further violence.

The shock of the First Partition spurred a period of profound national soul-searching and a desperate, final push for reform. The culmination of this effort was the Great Sejm, which convened from 1788 to 1792. Seizing an opportunity while Russia was distracted by wars with the Ottoman Empire and Sweden, the reformers worked to fundamentally restructure the state. The result was the Constitution of May 3, 1791, a revolutionary document that stands as Europe's first modern written constitution. The constitution transformed the Commonwealth into a hereditary constitutional monarchy, abolished the *liberum veto* and other dysfunctional aspects of the old system, and granted political rights to townspeople. A subsequent act, the "Mutual Pledge of the Two Nations," ensured that the Grand Duchy of Lithuania maintained its separate status and administrative structures within the reformed state.

This attempt at national rebirth was seen by Catherine the Great as an intolerable act of insubordination and a dangerous symptom of "Jacobin" revolutionary fever. Denouncing the constitution, she gave her backing to a group of reactionary Polish magnates who formed the Targowica Confederation to restore their old privileges. In 1792, a massive Russian army invaded to "support" the confederates in the War in Defense of the Constitution. The Commonwealth's army, though fighting bravely, was no match. King Stanisław August, hoping to save some remnant of the state, capitulated and joined the Targowica Confederation, a move that destroyed the morale of the reformers.

The aftermath was the Second Partition in 1793. This time, only Russia and Prussia took part. Prussia annexed Gdańsk and a large part of western Poland. Russia seized a vast swathe of the Grand Duchy of Lithuania, including the central Belarusian lands with the cities of Minsk, Slutsk, and Pinsk. The Commonwealth was reduced to a rump state, a pitiful fragment of its former self, and its last Sejm, convened at Grodno under the barrels of Russian guns, was forced to annul the May 3rd Constitution and approve the new dismemberment.

The final act was one of desperate, heroic resistance. In March 1794, the Kościuszko Uprising erupted. It was led by Tadeusz Kościuszko, a veteran of the American Revolutionary War and a native of the Brest region of Belarus. Proclaiming a national insurrection in Kraków, he fought not for the rights of a single class, but for the independence of the nation as a whole. The uprising quickly spread to the Grand Duchy of Lithuania, where it was led by the charismatic and politically radical Colonel Jakub Jasiński, a poet and engineer who led a successful insurrection to liberate Vilnius in April. For a brief moment, the spirit of revolution burned brightly. But the insurgents, armed with more passion than munitions, could not hold out against the professional armies of Russia and Prussia.

The uprising was crushed with overwhelming force. Russian General Alexander Suvorov stormed a suburb of Warsaw, carrying out a massacre that broke the will of the defenders. Kościuszko had been wounded and captured weeks earlier at the Battle of Maciejowice. With the failure of the uprising, the partitioning powers decided to solve the "Polish problem" once and for all.

On October 24, 1795, Russia, Prussia, and Austria signed the treaty for the Third Partition, erasing what was left of the Polish-Lithuanian Commonwealth from the map. Russia annexed the final remaining territories of the Grand Duchy of Lithuania, including Vilnius, Grodno, and Brest. The state that had been a major European power for centuries, a unique federal republic of nobles, had ceased to exist. Its lands, and the entire Belarusian population, were now under the dominion of foreign empires. For Belarus, this meant complete absorption into the Russian Empire, beginning a new and difficult chapter under the rule of the Tsars.

CHAPTER NINE: Life Under the Tsars: Russification and Resistance

The final partition of the Polish-Lithuanian Commonwealth in 1795 was not merely a redrawing of borders; it was the closing of a world. For the lands of Belarus, the absorption into the Russian Empire marked the beginning of a new epoch defined by the systematic effort of an imperial state to digest and reshape a society it viewed as fundamentally Russian, yet corrupted by centuries of Polish and Catholic influence. This process, known as Russification, was a top-down project of administrative, religious, and cultural engineering. It was met not with quiet acquiescence, but with waves of resistance, from the secret societies of university students to the desperate, bloody uprisings of a nobility clinging to the memory of their lost state.

Upon annexing the Belarusian lands, the Russian state set about dismantling the old administrative structures of the Grand Duchy of Lithuania. The territory was reorganized into Russian-style governorates (*guberniyas*), eventually including Minsk, Grodno, Vitebsk, and Mogilev, which were collectively administered as part of the "North-Western Territory" (*Severo-Zapadny Krai*). The name "Belarus" was officially used for a time but was later discouraged in favor of a designation that emphasized the region's place as a mere geographic appendage of the Russian core.

Initially, Catherine the Great adopted a pragmatic approach toward the local nobility, the *szlachta*. She offered to respect their property and privileges in exchange for an oath of loyalty, an offer most of the landed gentry, weary of war and chaos, accepted. The Russian imperial system, however, demanded a more rigid and verifiable hierarchy than the sprawling, often-undocumented nobility of the old Commonwealth. The *szlachta* were required to present formal proof of their noble status to imperial heraldic commissions, a bureaucratic ordeal that many of the poorer, landless gentry could not navigate. Thousands were consequently reclassified as state peasants or commoners, stripping them of their ancient rights and social standing.

The central pillar of imperial policy was the official ideology of "Orthodoxy, Autocracy, and Nationality," formulated under Tsar Nicholas I. According to this worldview, the East Slavs constituted a single "all-Russian" people, divided into three branches: Great Russians, Little Russians (Ukrainians), and White Russians (Belarusians). The historical narrative promoted from St. Petersburg held that the Belarusians were a long-lost branch of the Russian family, torn from the motherland by the Lithuanians and Poles, and that their reunion with the empire was a just and natural restoration. The goal of Tsarist policy, therefore, was to erase the cultural and religious distinctions that had developed over five centuries of separation.

A brief but significant interruption to this process came in 1812. When Napoleon Bonaparte's Grande Armée marched east, many in the former Grand Duchy greeted him as a liberator. The local nobility, dreaming of a restored Commonwealth or at least an autonomous Duchy, enthusiastically formed regiments to fight for the French emperor. This hope was short-lived. The devastating Russian campaign, the brutal retreat of the French, and the ultimate victory of Tsar Alexander I extinguished any prospect of renewed statehood. The collaboration with Napoleon only served to deepen the Russian state's suspicion of the western provinces and reinforced its determination to stamp out any lingering Polish loyalties.

The most potent tool of Russification was wielded against the dominant faith of the Belarusian peasantry: the Uniate Church. St. Petersburg viewed the Greek Catholic faith as a political and spiritual anomaly, a product of Polish intrigue that kept millions of Orthodox souls in communion with a foreign pope. A systematic campaign was launched to dismantle the church from within. The architect of this policy was Iosif Semashko, a Uniate priest who became a fervent advocate for "reunification" with the Russian Orthodox Church. Appointed to a key bishopric, Semashko worked for years, with the full backing of the state, to purge

Uniate rituals of their Latinized elements, replacing them with standard Russian Orthodox practices. Clergy who resisted were removed, and state funds were channeled to those who complied.

The final act came on February 12, 1839, at the Synod of Polotsk. Orchestrated by Semashko and two other bishops, the synod formally declared the Union of Brest null and void within the Russian Empire and petitioned Tsar Nicholas I to accept its clergy and faithful into the fold of the Russian Orthodox Church. The petition, signed by over 1,300 priests, was swiftly approved. With the stroke of a pen, the Uniate Church, which had been the faith of the majority of the population for over two centuries, ceased to legally exist. Over 1.6 million believers and 1,600 parishes were absorbed into the state church. While some priests and parishioners resisted, they were met with state coercion. This forced conversion was a transformative event, severing the peasantry's main institutional link with the culture of the old Commonwealth and reorienting their spiritual lives toward Moscow.

Resistance to Russian rule increasingly took the form of armed conspiracy, centered on the Polonized *szlachta* who yearned for the restoration of their lost homeland. The first major challenge erupted in November 1830. Sparked by a revolt of officer cadets in Warsaw, the November Uprising quickly spread to the Belarusian and Lithuanian lands. Across the region, the local gentry formed partisan units and took up arms against the imperial garrisons. However, the rebellion suffered from a fatal flaw: it was almost exclusively a project of the nobility. The insurgents' calls for a restored Poland failed to mobilize the peasantry, who were largely indifferent or hostile to the cause of their landlords. Lacking broad support and facing the overwhelming might of the Russian army, the uprising was crushed by the autumn of 1831.

The crackdown that followed was severe. Nicholas I was determined to punish the rebellious provinces and eradicate the Polish influence he blamed for the unrest. The estates of thousands of participating nobles were confiscated. The Polish language was banned from administration and the educational system, with

Russian made the compulsory language of instruction. The venerable Vilnius University, a hotbed of romantic nationalism and secret student societies like the Philomats and Filarets, was closed in 1832. This wave of repression was accompanied by the final abolition of the Third Statute of Lithuania in 1840, erasing the last legal vestige of the Grand Duchy and fully incorporating the region into the Russian imperial legal and administrative system.

One last, desperate bid for freedom came a generation later with the January Uprising of 1863–1864. Like its predecessor, it began in Warsaw and was led by the *szlachta*. Yet in the lands of Belarus and Lithuania, the rebellion took on a distinct character, thanks largely to one man: Konstanty Kalinowski, known to Belarusians as Kastuś. A young nobleman from the Grodno region, Kalinowski was a radical democrat who represented a new kind of resistance. He understood that a revolt of the gentry alone was doomed to fail.

To rally the peasantry, Kalinowski began publishing the first newspaper in the modern Belarusian language (using the Latin alphabet), *Mużyckaja prauda* ("Peasants' Truth"). In its seven issues, written in simple, direct language, he bypassed the lofty goal of restoring the old Commonwealth and instead addressed the peasants' immediate concerns. He argued that a just government would give them land and freedom, and he framed the fight not as a Polish cause, but as a struggle against the oppression of the Tsar in St. Petersburg. When the uprising began, Kalinowski became a leading figure of the underground Provisional Provincial Government of Lithuania and Belarus.

The uprising was a guerrilla war, fought by small, mobile bands of insurgents against a massive Russian army. Despite their bravery, they stood little chance. The Tsarist government, having emancipated the serfs in 1861, successfully co-opted the peasantry by offering them more favorable land terms than the rebels could promise. By the spring of 1864, the rebellion was brutally suppressed.

Kalinowski was captured in January 1864 and imprisoned in Vilnius. While awaiting execution, he wrote his defiant "Letters from Under the Gallows," a political testament smuggled out of his cell. In it, he made a final appeal to his people: "From under the gallows in Moscow, I am writing to you, people. Only then will you live happily, when no Muscovite is left over you." He was publicly hanged in a Vilnius square on March 22, 1864.

The man sent to crush the uprising and pacify the region was Governor-General Mikhail Muravyov, who earned the moniker "the Hangman" for his ruthless efficiency. Muravyov believed the root of the problem was the lingering Polish cultural and economic dominance. His policies after 1864 represented the zenith of Russification. Hundreds of insurgents were executed and thousands deported to Siberia. Polish was banned from all public use, and even speaking it in public places was forbidden. Catholic churches were closed or converted to Orthodox ones, and the construction of new Catholic churches was prohibited. To further sever ties with the West, Muravyov banned the printing of Belarusian texts in the Latin alphabet in 1864, a policy that stifled the nascent literary movement for decades. Simultaneously, he implemented policies designed to elevate the Orthodox Belarusian peasantry, viewing them as the local Russian element that needed to be protected from the Polonized Catholic gentry.

By the end of the 1860s, armed resistance had been definitively crushed. The old szlachta culture, which had defined the Belarusian lands for half a millennium, was broken. The policies of Muravyov had accelerated the integration of the region into the empire, cementing Russian political control and imposing the Russian language and the Orthodox faith. Yet, in the embers of the failed uprisings, a new idea had been kindled. The actions and writings of figures like Kalinowski, who had appealed directly to the peasantry in their own language, hinted at a form of identity that was neither Polish nor Russian.

CHAPTER TEN: The Birth of a National Idea: The 19th Century Cultural Revival

With the gallows in Vilnius's Lukiškės Square casting a long shadow over the future, the dream of restoring the Polish-Lithuanian Commonwealth through armed insurrection died with the last gasps of the 1863 Uprising. The old patriotism of the *szlachta*, rooted in the memory of a lost state and a shared political culture, was broken by Mikhail Muravyov's campaign of executions, deportations, and systematic Russification. For those who still harbored a sense of distinct identity in the North-Western Territory, it was clear that a new path had to be found. The battle for political independence was lost; the struggle for a soul had just begun. This new struggle would not be fought with swords and scythes in the forests, but with pens, printing presses, and the patient collection of folk songs. It was a quiet revolution that sought to define a nation not by its past political borders, but by the language, customs, and folklore of the peasantry who had for centuries been the silent foundation of the land.

The intellectual seeds for this shift were sown not in local conspiracies, but in the broader European movement of Romanticism. Sweeping across the continent, Romanticism championed the authentic, the ancient, and the emotional, finding true national spirit not in the polished culture of royal courts, but in the untamed folklore of the common people. This intellectual current inspired a new generation of scholars, poets, and amateur enthusiasts across the Belarusian lands to turn their attention to the villages. They began to look at the peasantry, long dismissed as an ignorant and backward mass, with new eyes, seeing them as living repositories of a unique and ancient heritage.

This ethnographic turn was often led by members of the Polonized gentry, men who were culturally Polish but deeply attached to the landscapes and people of their native land. Jan Czeczot, a friend of the great poet Adam Mickiewicz, was an early pioneer, wandering the countryside to meticulously collect thousands of Belarusian folk songs, which he published with Polish translations in the 1830s and 40s. His contemporary, Jan Barszczewski, drew on the dark, supernatural folklore of the Polotsk region for his collection of gothic tales, *Szlachcic Zawalnia, czyli Białoruś w fantastycznych opowiadaniach* ("The Nobleman Zawalnia, or Belarus in Fantastic Stories"). Though writing in Polish, these authors placed the Belarusian vernacular and worldview at the center of their work, presenting it to a wider audience as something worthy of literary attention. Even Mickiewicz himself, the national bard of Poland, wove the imagery, myths, and language of his Belarusian homeland near Navahrudak into the fabric of his epic poems, inadvertently preserving and elevating the very culture the imperial state sought to either ignore or absorb.

The heart of this emerging national idea was the question of language. For centuries, the speech of the Belarusian lands had been derided from all sides. To the Polish elite, it was a coarse rural patois; to the Russian authorities, it was a "spoiled" dialect of Great Russian. It was the language of the hearth and the field, but it had no official status and a very limited literary tradition. The challenge was to prove it could be a language of art and ideas. A crucial first step came with the anonymous burlesque poems *Eneida navyvarat* ("Aeneid Inside Out") and *Taras na Parnase* ("Taras on Parnassus"), which began circulating in handwritten copies in the first half of the century. By humorously placing Belarusian peasants into the world of classical mythology, these works demonstrated the language's expressive power, vitality, and wit, becoming wildly popular and proving that the vernacular could carry a sophisticated literary narrative.

The man who took on the task of building a modern Belarusian literature was Vintsent Dunin-Martsinkyevich. A playwright, poet, and translator of noble birth, he made the audacious choice to write in the language of his peasants. His works, staged by a traveling troupe he created, were often bilingual, a reflection of the society he depicted. In his popular comic opera *Sielanka* ("The Idyll"), the gentry characters spoke and sang in Polish, while the peasants used Belarusian, a device that faithfully captured the region's linguistic reality. In his most famous play, *Pinskaya shlyakhta* ("The Pinsk Gentry"), he satirized the airs and pretensions of the petty nobility, using their often-comical mixture of Polish and Belarusian to great effect. Dunin-Martsinkyevich's work was a landmark; it legitimized the Belarusian language as a medium for the stage and for print, creating a small but vital body of modern literature where none had existed before.

Ironically, the most intensive efforts to study Belarusian culture came as a direct consequence of the very policies designed to erase it. After the 1863 Uprising, Governor-General Muravyov's administration pursued a strategy of "dis-Polonizing" the region by emphasizing the "primordially Russian" character of the Orthodox Belarusian peasantry. To prove this thesis, the imperial government sponsored a wave of ethnographic research. Russian scholars, teachers, and officials were dispatched to the North-Western Territory to document the local culture, confident that they would find evidence of an unblemished Russian soul.

What they found was something far more complex. Pavel Shein, a Russian teacher sent to Belarus, became one of the most important folklorists of the century. Driven by an almost obsessive passion for collecting, he spent decades compiling a monumental, multi-volume work titled *Materials for the Study of the Life and Language of the Russian Population in the North-Western Territory*. Despite its imperial framing, the work was a treasure trove, a vast and systematically organized collection of Belarusian wedding rituals, folk songs, proverbs, and incantations. By preserving the raw material of the culture in such detail, Shein inadvertently provided future Belarusian nationalists with an encyclopedic resource to argue for its distinctiveness.

Similarly, the work of Yefim Karsky, a philologist from Grodno, laid the scientific foundation for Belarusian linguistics. His magnum opus, the seven-volume *The Belarusians*, published in the early 20th century, was the first comprehensive academic study of the Belarusian language, its dialects, and its literature. While Karsky remained a loyal subject of the empire and viewed Belarusian as part of the broader Russian linguistic family, his rigorous scholarship provided incontrovertible proof of its unique phonetic, grammatical, and lexical features. He had set out to map a branch of the Russian tree, but in doing so, he had drawn its borders so clearly that it could be seen as a forest in its own right.

By the last two decades of the 19th century, this cultural raw material began to be shaped into a coherent political ideology by a new generation of activists. These were not the Polonized gentry of the old Commonwealth, but a new intelligentsia, often the sons of peasants or priests who had made their way through the Russian university system. Influenced by the revolutionary ideas of Populism (*Narodnichestvo*) circulating in St. Petersburg and Moscow, they came to believe that their duty was to serve "the people," and for them, "the people" were the Belarusian-speaking peasantry.

Clandestine student circles began to form. In the 1880s, a group in St. Petersburg calling itself "Homan" ("The Din") published a hectographed journal that, for the first time, began to articulate a clear political program. They argued that the Belarusians were a distinct nation, separate from both Poles and Russians, and that they deserved, at minimum, autonomy within a federalized Russian state.

The most powerful and influential voice to emerge from this movement was that of Frantsishak Bahushevich. A lawyer by profession and a participant in the 1863 Uprising in his youth, Bahushevich was forced to live in exile for many years. Under the pseudonyms Maciej Buračok and Symon Reuka, he published two small collections of poetry abroad in the 1890s: *Dudka biełaruskaja* ("Belarusian Pipe") and *Smyk biełaruski* ("Belarusian Fiddle"). The poems themselves were simple, drawing on the hardships and rhythms of peasant life. Their true significance, however, lay in their prefaces.

In the preface to the *Dudka*, Bahushevich penned what would become the manifesto of the national revival. He addressed his people directly, urging them to cherish their language as the ultimate hallmark of their nationhood. He decried those who called their language "churlish" and dismissed it as a mere dialect. "Our language," he declared, "is as human and noble as French, German, or any other." He painted a brief history of the Belarusian people, invoking the Grand Duchy of Lithuania and the Statutes written in Old Belarusian to give his peasant audience a sense of a proud, independent past. He concluded with a line that would echo for generations: "Do not forsake our language, lest you die!" (*Nie pakidajcie ž movy našaj biełaruskaj, kab nie ŭmiorli!*).

This was a radical act. Bahushevich was the first to explicitly and popularly link language, identity, and national survival. He provided the nascent movement with its foundational text and its most enduring slogan. He took the ethnographic raw material collected by scholars and the literary experiments of poets and fused them into a passionate call for national consciousness.

As the 19th century drew to a close, the Belarusian national movement was still in its infancy. It was a cause championed by a tiny circle of intellectuals, largely unknown to the millions of peasants whose identity they sought to define. The majority of the rural population, when asked who they were, would still reply that they were *tuteishy*—"locals." Their world was circumscribed by their village, their primary loyalty was to their faith—Orthodox or Catholic—and their political consciousness was minimal. Yet, the groundwork had been laid. A modern literary language was being forged, a unique cultural heritage had been documented, a historical narrative was being constructed, and a passionate argument for the existence of a Belarusian nation had been made. The intellectual tinder was dry; all that was needed was the spark of the political and social upheavals of the new century to set it ablaze.

CHAPTER ELEVEN: The Tumult of the Early 20th Century: World War I and the Struggle for Independence

The dawn of the twentieth century found the Belarusian national idea in a state of fragile potential. It was an idea nurtured by a handful of intellectuals, whispered in clandestine student groups, and cryptically expressed in poems published abroad. For the vast majority of the peasants in the Russian Empire's North-Western Territory, the primary markers of identity remained local—being *tuteishy*, or "from here"—and religious. Yet, the accumulated cultural and linguistic work of the 19th century had created a foundation. What the movement desperately needed was an opening, a crack in the monolithic structure of the Tsarist autocracy that would allow these ideas to reach the people. That crack appeared in 1905.

The Russian Revolution of 1905, sparked by the Bloody Sunday massacre in St. Petersburg, was a wave of mass political and social unrest that shook the empire to its core. Though its epicenters were the great industrial cities and naval bases, its tremors were felt throughout the Belarusian lands. Workers in Minsk and Vitebsk went on strike, peasants revolted against landlords, and soldiers mutinied. Faced with the potential collapse of his regime, Tsar Nicholas II issued the October Manifesto, a reluctant concession that granted civil liberties, including freedom of speech and assembly, and established an elected parliament, the Duma.

This brief political thaw provided the oxygen the Belarusian national movement needed to ignite. The new freedoms, however circumscribed, allowed for the creation of the first legal political organizations and publications. The most important of these was the Belarusian Socialist Hramada (Assembly), a party that combined socialist ideals of land reform and workers' rights with a call for national autonomy within a federal Russian republic. Its leaders, brothers Ivan and Anton Lutskevich, Vaclau Lastouski, and Alaiza Pashkevich (better known by her pen name, Ciotka), were part of a new, politically astute generation of activists.

Even more significant was the birth of the first legal, mass-circulation Belarusian-language newspaper, *Nasha Niva* ("Our Field"), which began publishing in Vilnius in November 1906. For the next decade, this weekly newspaper would be the heart, soul, and brain of the national movement. Under the editorship of figures like Aliaksandr Ulasau, *Nasha Niva* became a hub for every aspiring Belarusian writer, poet, and public intellectual. It was on its pages that the literary talents of Yanka Kupala and Yakub Kolas, who would become the twin pillars of modern Belarusian literature, first blossomed. The paper meticulously worked to standardize the modern Belarusian language, promoted a secular and distinct national identity, and painstakingly reported on the life of the Belarusian village, giving its peasant readers a sense of a shared experience and destiny. The entire period of national development from 1906 to 1915 would become known as the "Nasha Niva Period," a testament to its profound impact.

This fragile spring of national life was trampled by the boots of marching armies. In August 1914, the Russian Empire entered the First World War. The Belarusian lands, situated on the empire's western frontier, were immediately placed under martial law. Initially, the region served as a crucial rear base for the Russian army, with the Supreme Commander's headquarters, the Stavka, located first at Baranovichi and later at Mogilev. But the war itself, a distant conflict in East Prussia and Galicia, came crashing home in the summer of 1915.

A massive German offensive, known as the Great Retreat, shattered the Russian front, forcing a chaotic and devastating withdrawal. As the Russian army fell back, it implemented a brutal scorched-earth policy, destroying anything that might be of use to the advancing enemy. This was compounded by a policy of forced resettlement. The military command, deeply suspicious of the loyalty of the local population, particularly Catholics and Jews, encouraged and often coerced civilians to flee eastward. This triggered a massive humanitarian catastrophe known as the *bezhanstva*, or refugee exodus. More than 1.4 million people, mostly Orthodox believers, abandoned their homes, clogging the roads in a desperate flight from the war.

By the autumn of 1915, the front line stabilized, carving Belarus in two. The new front stretched roughly along a line from Dvinsk (Daugavpils) in the north, through Postavy and Smorgon, down to Baranovichi and Pinsk. This brutal gash across the country would remain for the next two and a half years, a zone of static, attritional trench warfare. Towns on the front line, like Smorgon, were utterly obliterated after holding out for 810 days of shelling and attacks.

The two parts of Belarus now lived under vastly different realities. In the eastern part, which remained under Russian control, life was dominated by the military. The region was flooded with soldiers and the remnants of the refugee population. Civilian life was subject to the harsh demands of martial law, and the national movement was driven underground once more. *Nasha Niva* was forced to cease publication.

In the west, the population found itself under German military occupation. This territory was incorporated into a vast administrative zone known as Ober Ost (Supreme Command of All German Forces in the East), ruled by the iron-fisted tandem of Field Marshal Paul von Hindenburg and General Erich Ludendorff. The primary goal of the German administration was the systematic exploitation of the region's economic resources for the German war effort. However, the Germans also pursued a political strategy of encouraging non-Russian nationalism to undermine any future Russian claim to the territory. For the Belarusian activists who had remained in Vilnius, this presented a strange and complex opportunity. While wary of their occupiers, they were able to secure a degree of tolerance for cultural work. Under strict German control, they opened Belarusian-language schools and relief organizations for war victims.

The event that shattered this stalemate was the February Revolution of 1917 in Russia. The sudden collapse of the Tsarist monarchy and the establishment of a Provisional Government in Petrograd created a power vacuum that electrified the political landscape across the former empire. In Minsk, which now became the center of political gravity for the national movement, Belarusian activists emerged from the shadows. The Belarusian Socialist Hramada and other groups organized themselves into a coordinating body, the Belarusian National Committee.

Throughout 1917, these nascent national organizations tried to navigate the revolutionary chaos. They sought recognition from the Russian Provisional Government, lobbied for autonomy, and competed for influence with the far more powerful and better-organized forces that were coming to dominate the region: the Russian military, the local councils (Soviets) of workers and soldiers heavily influenced by the Bolsheviks, and Polish groups that dreamed of incorporating these lands into a restored Poland. The Belarusian movement, still largely confined to the intelligentsia, struggled to make its voice heard.

The Bolshevik seizure of power in the October Revolution of 1917 radically changed the situation again. The Bolsheviks' promise of "self-determination for all nations" of the former empire seemed to offer a path to statehood. To seize this opportunity and provide a definitive answer to the question of Belarus's future, the leaders of the national movement took their boldest step yet. In December 1917, they convened the First All-Belarusian Congress in Minsk.

It was a remarkable gathering, the first truly representative assembly in the nation's history. Some 1,872 delegates arrived from every corner of the Belarusian lands—from the German-occupied west and the Russian-controlled east, from the refugee communities in Russia, and from the Belarusian soldiers' councils on the crumbling front. For thirteen days, in the hall of the Minsk City Theatre, the delegates—representing a wide spectrum of political views—heatedly debated their future. Right-leaning delegates from the west, having experienced German occupation, pushed for immediate and full independence. More left-leaning delegates from the east argued for broad autonomy within a democratic Russian federation.

Despite the divisions, the will to forge a common path was strong. The Congress elected a 71-member Council, a proto-parliament, to act as the executive body for the creation of a Belarusian state. In the early hours of December 18, the delegates began to pass a resolution, proclaiming the right of the Belarusian people to self-determination and the establishment of a democratic republic.

At that decisive moment, the doors of the theatre burst open. Bolshevik soldiers, acting on the orders of the local Soviet military authorities who viewed the Congress as a "counter-revolutionary" challenge to their power, stormed the hall. The presidium was arrested, and the delegates were violently dispersed. The first attempt at democratic self-governance was crushed by force. But the act of dispersal had the opposite of its intended effect. It radicalized many of the moderate delegates and created a core of determined leaders who now saw no future in any arrangement with the Bolsheviks. The Council elected by the Congress went underground, ready to bide its time. The dream of statehood, though violently interrupted, was not extinguished; it was merely waiting for the next tremor in the earthquake of war and revolution to find its moment to be declared to the world.

CHAPTER TWELVE: The Belarusian People's Republic: A Brief Glimmer of Statehood

The Bolshevik soldiers who stormed the Minsk City Theatre in December 1917 and dispersed the First All-Belarusian Congress may have believed they had extinguished the nascent flame of Belarusian statehood. In reality, they had only scattered its embers. The act of suppression galvanized the national leaders, convincing them that any hope of autonomy within a Russian state, Bolshevik or otherwise, was a dangerous illusion. The Council elected by the Congress simply went underground, its executive committee becoming a government-in-waiting, watching the chaotic interplay of great powers and waiting for a moment to reassert itself. That moment arrived with the speed and force of a German military train.

The peace negotiations at Brest-Litovsk between the new Bolshevik government and the Central Powers had stalled by early 1918. Leon Trotsky, the Soviet negotiator, was attempting a novel diplomatic strategy of "no war, no peace," hoping to prolong the talks until a proletarian revolution erupted in Germany. The German High Command, losing patience, opted for a more traditional approach. On February 18, 1918, they launched Operation Faustschlag ("Fist Punch"), a massive offensive along the entire Eastern Front. The demoralized and disintegrating Russian army offered virtually no resistance. German troops advanced with astonishing speed, often traveling by rail, in what one German general called "the most comical war I have ever known."

For the Bolsheviks in Minsk, the game was up. Faced with the unstoppable German advance, their local administration packed its bags and fled eastward. Minsk was left in a state of limbo, a city without a government. Into this power vacuum stepped the underground Executive Committee of the All-Belarusian

Congress. On February 21, 1918, just hours before the first German cavalry patrols entered the city, the committee emerged from hiding and issued its First Constituent Charter. In this bold document, it declared itself the temporary authority in the land, styling itself the People's Secretariat of Belarus. The first, tentative step toward statehood had been taken.

The arrival of the German army created a deeply ambiguous and uncomfortable reality. The activists of the national movement were not pro-German, but they were staunchly anti-Bolshevik and anti-Russian imperialist. The Germans, for their part, had little genuine interest in Belarusian independence. Their primary goal was to secure the resources of the occupied territories and create a buffer zone against Russia. Still, they pursued a policy of tolerating and sometimes encouraging local national movements as a way to weaken Russian influence. For the People's Secretariat, this meant they were allowed to exist and operate within Minsk, but they wielded no real power. They were sovereigns without sovereignty, a government under the watchful eye of a foreign military administration.

This precarious situation was thrown into sharp relief by events back at the negotiating table. On March 3, 1918, the Bolsheviks, facing the complete collapse of their front, finally signed the punitive Treaty of Brest-Litovsk. Under its harsh terms, Soviet Russia renounced its claims to vast territories, including Poland, Lithuania, and Ukraine. Most of the Belarusian lands were formally ceded to German control, effectively partitioning the nation and treating its territory as a simple bargaining chip between two great powers.

For the leaders in Minsk, the treaty was an outrage, a confirmation that neither Berlin nor Moscow had any regard for Belarusian self-determination. It served as the final catalyst. On March 9, the Council issued its Second Constituent Charter. This document was more assertive, officially proclaiming the establishment of the Belarusian People's Republic (BNR) and outlining the fundamental rights and freedoms of its citizens. It declared freedom of speech, press, and assembly; it abolished private ownership of land and established an eight-hour workday. It was a progressive, democratic vision for a state that did not yet fully exist.

The final, decisive step came in response to the treaty that had ignored them. Debates raged within the Rada, the expanded council that now served as the BNR's parliament. Some members, particularly those with socialist leanings, were wary of severing all ties with Russia. Others argued that the Treaty of Brest-Litovsk had freed them from any obligation to Moscow and that only a declaration of full independence could assert their legitimacy on the world stage.

On the night of March 24-25, 1918, in a tense session held in Minsk, the independence faction won the day. The Rada of the BNR adopted the Third Constituent Charter, its declaration of independence. The document declared the Belarusian People's Republic a "free and independent state" and pronounced the Treaty of Brest-Litovsk null and void in regards to Belarus. It laid claim to all lands where Belarusians constituted a majority, including the regions of Mogilev, Minsk, Vitebsk, and the Belarusian parts of the Grodno, Vilnius, Smolensk, and Chernihiv governorates. The date, March 25th, would henceforth be celebrated by independence advocates as Freedom Day (*Dzień Voli*), the birthday of the modern Belarusian state.

Having declared independence, the government of the BNR, led by Prime Minister Jazep Varonka, faced the monumental task of turning a declaration into a functioning state. The challenges were immense. The BNR had no army, no police force, no treasury, and its claimed territory was under the firm control of the German military. The German authorities refused to grant the BNR official recognition, viewing it merely as a local representative committee, not a sovereign government. In April 1918, they went so far as to ban the People's Secretariat, though they allowed the Rada to continue its activities.

Despite these constraints, the BNR's leaders worked tirelessly to build the institutions of statehood. They established a skeletal administration, attempted to organize local government, and, most successfully, focused on cultural and educational work. Over 350 Belarusian-language schools were opened, newspapers began to be published, and a national theatre was founded. The government also adopted the symbols that would become enduring emblems of Belarusian independence: the ancient coat of arms, the Pahonia—a charging knight on horseback—and a white-red-white striped flag. These symbols, rooted in the history of the Grand Duchy of Lithuania, were a deliberate rejection of Russian imperial iconography and a claim to a distinct historical heritage.

The BNR also made a concerted effort to gain international recognition. Diplomatic missions were dispatched to neighboring countries and the major European capitals. They managed to secure a degree of de facto recognition from Ukraine and Finland. A key objective was to persuade the government in Berlin to change its stance. In April 1918, the Rada sent a telegram to Kaiser Wilhelm II, thanking him for the "liberation" of Belarus and expressing the hope that Germany would support its independence. This move was deeply controversial, causing a split within the Rada and alienating socialist members who saw it as an unacceptable appeal to an imperial power. The Kaiser never replied.

The state that existed more on paper and in the hearts of its founders than on the ground was ultimately a hostage to the outcome of the Great War. The fate of the BNR was sealed in the west, on the battlefields of France. In November 1918, Germany signed the Armistice, admitting defeat. The Treaty of Brest-Litovsk was annulled. As the demoralized German army began its slow withdrawal from the occupied territories, a power vacuum once again opened.

This time, however, there was no doubt about who would fill it. The Bolsheviks in Moscow had never recognized the BNR, viewing it as a "counter-revolutionary" puppet state. As the Germans retreated westward, the newly formed Red Army advanced from the east. The meager, poorly organized military units of the BNR were no match for the disciplined Bolshevik forces.

In December 1918, with the Red Army closing in, the Rada and the government of the Belarusian People's Republic abandoned Minsk. They moved first to Vilnius, then to Hrodna, trying to maintain a foothold on Belarusian soil. But the tide of the Russian Civil War was against them. By January 1919, the Bolsheviks were in firm control of Minsk, where they promptly established the Byelorussian Soviet Socialist Republic.

The leaders of the BNR were forced into exile. The brief, nine-month glimmer of statehood on Belarusian land was over. Yet, the BNR was not entirely extinguished. Its governing body, the Rada, continued to function abroad, becoming one of the world's longest-surviving governments-in-exile. While it had failed to secure a permanent, independent state, the BNR had created a powerful precedent. It had made the first formal declaration of Belarusian sovereignty in the modern era, adopted national symbols, and established the principle of an independent Belarusian state in the minds of a generation of activists. The idea, once declared, could not be un-declared.

CHAPTER THIRTEEN: In the Soviet Crucible: The Formation of the BSSR

As the German army packed its baggage and retreated westward in the dying days of 1918, a new force was marching in from the east to fill the vacuum. For the fledgling government of the Belarusian People's Republic (BNR), this was the end. Fleeing Minsk just ahead of the advancing Red Army, they were destined for a long and politically fruitless life in exile. For the Bolsheviks, however, the arrival of their troops in the Belarusian lands was not a simple act of conquest, but the beginning of a complex and often contradictory experiment in state-building. The challenge they faced was how to impose a proletarian dictatorship on a territory where a rival national government had just declared independence, without appearing to be just another incarnation of the old Russian imperialists they had so vocally condemned.

Their solution was a masterstroke of political pragmatism, a direct application of Lenin's nationality policy. This doctrine, designed to win the support of the non-Russian peoples of the former empire, offered a tantalizing promise: self-determination. In practice, this meant creating states that were "national in form, socialist in content." The Bolsheviks would counter the "bourgeois nationalism" of the BNR not by denying the existence of a Belarusian nation, but by creating their own version of it—a Soviet one. This strategy allowed them to co-opt the powerful idea of nationhood while ensuring that ultimate political control remained firmly in Moscow. The Belarusian people would be granted a republic, but it would be a republic forged in the Soviet crucible.

The first moves were made with bureaucratic swiftness. On December 30, 1918, a conference of the North-Western Regional Committee of the Russian Communist Party convened in Smolensk. Acting on instructions from Moscow, the delegates declared themselves the First Congress of the Communist Party of Byelorussia. On January 1, 1919, they issued a manifesto formally proclaiming the creation of the Socialist Soviet Republic of Byelorussia (SSRB).

The new republic was, on paper, vast. Its territory was defined along the broad ethnic lines claimed by the earlier national movement, encompassing the governorates of Minsk, Mogilev, Grodno, Vitebsk, and Smolensk. Its first government was headed by the Belarusian writer Zmicier Zhylunovich (known by his literary pseudonym, Ciška Hartny), a figure with genuine national credentials. The head of the Central Executive Committee was the veteran Armenian Bolshevik, Alexander Miasnikian, a man who, ironically, had previously been an opponent of Belarusian autonomy. For a few days, the capital of this new Soviet Belarus was Smolensk, an ancient city with deep historical ties to the region. Then, as the Red Army secured Minsk, the government relocated.

The sovereignty of this new republic, however, proved to be exceptionally fragile. Moscow's grant of self-determination came with fine print, and the ink was barely dry on the proclamation before it was amended. On January 16, 1919, just two weeks after its grand unveiling, the Central Committee of the Russian Communist Party in Moscow made a stunning decision. The eastern provinces of Vitebsk, Mogilev, and Smolensk—economically valuable and with significant Russian populations—were to be detached from the SSRB and incorporated directly into the Russian Soviet Federative Socialist Republic (RSFSR). This act of political surgery, performed without any consultation with the supposed government in Minsk, reduced the new republic to a shadow of its proclaimed self, comprising only the Minsk and Grodno regions. It was a stark and early lesson in the realities of power within the emerging Soviet system: national republics were welcome to exist, but their borders and their authority were subject to the strategic interests of the center.

What was left of the SSRB was then immediately repurposed for a new geopolitical gambit. As the Red Army continued its westward advance, it came into direct conflict with the forces of a newly resurrected Poland. The Polish state, reborn after more than a century of partition, had its own ambitious plans for the region, inspired by the historical borders of the Polish-Lithuanian Commonwealth. With the Polish army advancing from the west, the Bolsheviks needed a buffer. The solution was to merge their two newest, weakest creations. On February 27, 1919, the rump SSRB was officially combined with the equally new Lithuanian Soviet Socialist Republic to form the Lithuanian-Byelorussian Soviet Socialist Republic, commonly known as Litbel.

Litbel was a curious and short-lived political hybrid. Its capital was established in Vilnius, and its government was a mix of Lithuanian and Belarusian communists, led by the Lithuanian Vincas Mickevičius-Kapsukas. The state was designed with a clear purpose: to act as a shield, absorbing the initial shock of the Polish advance and preventing a direct war between Warsaw and Moscow. It was also an attempt to create a political entity in a region of deeply mixed ethnicity, a Soviet answer to the old Grand Duchy of Lithuania. The new government went out of its way to avoid promoting any specific national identity, focusing instead on class war and the implementation of harsh "War Communism" policies, which involved the forced requisition of grain from a resentful peasantry.

The existence of Litbel was as chaotic as it was brief. It was a government on the run. In April 1919, Polish forces under Józef Piłsudski captured its capital, Vilnius. The government of Litbel fled to Minsk. In August, Minsk too fell to the Poles. The government retreated to Smolensk, but by then it was a government in name only. After less than six months of harried existence, the buffer state had been all but erased by the Polish army. The first Soviet attempt to institutionalize a Belarusian state, in both its initial and amalgamated forms, had collapsed.

For the next year, the Belarusian lands became the primary battleground of the Polish-Soviet War. This was not a war of clear front lines and decisive battles, but a brutal, seesawing conflict that laid waste to the countryside. For the local population, caught between the Polish "Whites" and the Bolshevik "Reds," it was a period of terror and confusion. Both sides conscripted local men, requisitioned food and horses, and executed suspected collaborators. The war had a devastating impact, compounding the destruction of the First World War and leaving a legacy of ruin and bitterness.

The tide of the war turned dramatically in the summer of 1920. The Red Army, having reorganized and concentrated its forces, launched a massive counter-offensive. Led by the ambitious young commander Mikhail Tukhachevsky, the Soviet Western Front smashed through the Polish lines. The advance was stunningly rapid. On July 11, 1920, Bolshevik forces retook Minsk. As they continued their seemingly unstoppable march on Warsaw, convinced that the workers of Poland were ready to rise up and join the revolution, the political future of Belarus was once again on the agenda.

With Minsk back in their hands, the Bolsheviks moved to re-establish a Soviet government. On July 31, 1920, the Belarusian Soviet Socialist Republic (BSSR) was proclaimed for a second time. This new BSSR, however, was a pale imitation of the one declared eighteen months earlier. It was a tiny entity, consisting of just six districts centered on Minsk, a sliver of territory in the heart of the Belarusian lands. Its existence was conditional, its future dependent entirely on the outcome of the war that was raging to its west.

That outcome was decided in mid-August, at the gates of Warsaw. In what the Poles would call the "Miracle on the Vistula," Piłsudski's forces, exploiting a gap in the Soviet lines, launched a desperate and brilliant counter-attack that routed Tukhachevsky's overextended armies. The Red Army, which had been on the verge of exporting revolution into Central Europe, was now in a state of chaotic retreat. The Poles pursued them eastward, retaking vast swathes of Belarusian and Ukrainian territory.

The war finally ground to a halt with both sides exhausted. Peace negotiations, which had started and stalled in Minsk, were moved to the neutral city of Riga, Latvia. There, Polish and Soviet Russian delegations hammered out the future of Eastern Europe.

Conspicuously absent from the negotiating table were any representatives of the Belarusian people. A delegation from the BNR government-in-exile was in Riga but was ignored by all parties. The delegation from the Soviet BSSR was present, but only as a powerless adjunct to the Russian delegation led by Adolph Joffe; when a Belarusian delegate tried to speak, he was told that the peace was being made with Poland, not Belarus.

The Treaty of Riga, signed on March 18, 1921, formalized the partition of Belarus. A new border was drawn, slicing through the historic Belarusian lands. The western half, including the cities of Grodno, Brest, and the cultural center of Vilnius, was incorporated into the new Polish Republic. The eastern half remained under Soviet control. The border was a line of political convenience, not ethnographic reality. It cut through villages, separated families, and placed a hard international frontier in the middle of a culturally contiguous area.

The re-established Byelorussian Soviet Socialist Republic was thus confirmed in its diminutive form. It was a state born of geopolitical calculation, shrunk by administrative fiat, dissolved, reborn in the heat of battle, and finally given its lasting borders by a treaty in which its people had no say. This small republic, comprising just the six central districts, was one of the four founding members to sign the treaty creating the Union of Soviet Socialist Republics on December 30, 1922. Its entry into this new federal union marked the end of the chaotic and violent period of its formation. The BSSR had been forged, hammered, and quenched in the crucible of war and revolution, emerging as a constituent, and subordinate, part of a much larger ideological experiment.

CHAPTER FOURTEEN: The Interwar Years: Industrialization, Collectivization, and Repression

The Byelorussian Soviet Socialist Republic, as confirmed by the Treaty of Riga, was a peculiar creation. It was a sliver of a state, covering just six districts around Minsk, a national republic whose titular population mostly lived outside its borders in Poland or in adjacent Russian provinces. To many, it seemed a temporary and barely viable entity. Yet, over the course of the 1920s, this rump state would undergo a remarkable transformation. Through a delicate interplay of cultural revival and brutal social engineering, Soviet Belarus would first be enlarged and encouraged to discover its national voice, only to have that voice systematically and violently silenced.

The first decade of the BSSR's existence unfolded under the umbrella of two crucial, union-wide policies. The first was the New Economic Policy (NEP), a pragmatic retreat from the harsh doctrines of War Communism, which allowed for a degree of market activity and private enterprise. For the war-ravaged Belarusian countryside, it provided a desperately needed breathing space, allowing agricultural production to slowly recover. The second, and more consequential for national identity, was the policy of *Korenizatsiya*, or "indigenization." This was Moscow's strategy to embed Soviet power in non-Russian republics by promoting local languages, cultures, and personnel. In Belarus, this policy became known as Belarusianization (*Belarusizatsyia*).

Belarusianization, officially launched in 1924, was a state-sponsored cultural revolution. The Belarusian language, long dismissed as a peasant dialect, was elevated to the official language of the republic. Government business, party congresses, and education were all to be conducted in Belarusian. A massive campaign was launched to teach the language to civil servants, many of whom were Russian, Jewish, or Polonized and had to attend mandatory language courses. By 1927, an impressive 80% of the republic's officials were reportedly fluent in Belarusian. The policy transformed education, with some 80% of schools switching to Belarusian as the primary language of instruction by 1928.

This policy was accompanied by a significant territorial expansion that gave the BSSR credibility as a genuine national unit. Moscow, eager to win the loyalties of Belarusians living under Polish rule in the west, decided to enlarge the republic. In 1924, and again in 1926, large territories with predominantly Belarusian populations were transferred from the Russian SFSR to the BSSR. These included the historic regions of Vitebsk, Polotsk, and Gomel. The enlargements more than doubled the republic's territory and population, transforming it from a tiny Minsk-based enclave into a substantial state of over four and a half million people.

This period saw an explosion of cultural and scholarly activity in Minsk, which became the undisputed center of the Belarusian national idea. The Institute of Belarusian Culture (Inbelkult), established in 1922, was upgraded to the Belarusian Academy of Sciences in 1928. It became the headquarters for a generation of intellectuals—historians, linguists, and writers—who eagerly set about the task of codifying the language, writing the first national histories, and publishing the works of a burgeoning literary scene. For many former activists from the short-lived Belarusian People's Republic who returned from exile, it seemed as though the cultural goals of their movement were being realized, albeit under a Red flag.

This "golden age" of Soviet Belarusian culture, however, was built on a foundation of political sand. As the 1920s drew to a close, Joseph Stalin consolidated his power in Moscow and prepared to launch the Soviet Union on a radically different course. The NEP was abandoned in favor of a new, ruthless drive for rapid and total transformation from above. In 1928, the first of the Five-Year Plans was launched. Its twin goals were forced-draft industrialization and the complete collectivization of agriculture.

For Belarus, as for the rest of the USSR, this marked the beginning of the "Great Break."

Industrialization aimed to turn a backward agrarian society into a modern industrial powerhouse in the span of a decade. Stalin's famous dictum, "We are fifty or a hundred years behind the advanced countries. We must make up this gap in ten years. Either we do it or they will crush us," set the frantic pace. In Belarus, which lacked significant mineral resources, the focus was not on the massive steel mills of the Urals but on developing existing industries and expanding the manufacturing base. New factories sprang up to produce machine tools, textiles, and wood products. The harvester factory in Gomel, founded in 1930, was a flagship project of this era. This drive created a new urban working class, as hundreds of thousands of peasants left their villages to work on the new construction sites and in the factories, fundamentally altering the republic's social structure.

The social cost of this industrial leap was immense, but it was dwarfed by the catastrophe unfolding in the countryside. Stalin's second revolution was the policy of collectivization, a brutal campaign to eradicate private farming and force the peasantry into large, state-controlled collective farms, or *kolkhozes*. The policy had two main objectives: to gain state control over grain production to feed the new industrial cities and to break the back of the independent peasantry, which the party viewed as a bastion of capitalism and a potential threat to its power.

The campaign was framed as a class war against the so-called *kulaks*, or wealthy peasants. In reality, any peasant who resisted giving up their land, livestock, and equipment could be branded a kulak. The policy of "dekulakization" was unleashed in 1929, with party activists and squads of urban workers sent into the villages to enforce the new order. Peasants who resisted were arrested, their property confiscated, and entire families deported to the frozen wastes of Siberia or Central Asia. The exact numbers are unknown, but it is estimated that hundreds of thousands in Belarus suffered this fate.

The remaining population was herded into the kolkhozes, often with only the clothes on their backs. The result was chaos and a collapse in agricultural output. Desperate peasants slaughtered their livestock rather than hand it over to the collective. The state, however, was determined to meet its grain procurement quotas at any cost. Brigades were sent to seize grain from the kolkhozes, often leaving the farmers with nothing to eat. While Belarus did not suffer the horrific, genocidal famine of the Holodomor in Ukraine, the years of 1932-33 brought widespread hunger, malnutrition, and death to its villages. Resistance was widespread but futile; peasant uprisings were brutally crushed by the OGPU, the state security police. By the mid-1930s, the battle for the countryside was over. The traditional village way of life had been destroyed, and the peasantry was effectively transformed into a rural proletariat, bound to the collective farm in a new form of serfdom.

The violence of collectivization and the frantic pace of industrialization were mirrored by a new, terrifying turn in the political sphere. The cultural flowering of Belarusianization was suddenly deemed a threat. The national intelligentsia, which had been so carefully nurtured in the 1920s, was now accused of being a hotbed of "bourgeois nationalism" and counter-revolution. The very people who had implemented the party's policy of Belarusianization were now its primary victims.

The first major blow came in 1930 with the fabrication of the "Union for the Liberation of Belarus" case. The OGPU announced the discovery of a vast, underground anti-Soviet organization supposedly plotting to separate the BSSR from the USSR with the help of Poland. It was a complete fiction, but it served as the pretext for a massive purge of the national intelligentsia. Over 100 prominent figures—academicians, writers, former government officials, and teachers—were arrested. Public show trials were planned but eventually scrapped; the accused were sentenced administratively to long terms in the Gulag or internal exile. The message was clear: the era of cultural tolerance was over.

What followed was a systematic dismantling of the achievements of the previous decade. The Belarusian language itself came under attack. A 1933 "reform" of Belarusian grammar and orthography was implemented, which artificially moved the language closer to Russian, purging it of distinctive features that were now deemed "nationalist" and "Polonizing." The policy of Belarusianization was quietly reversed, and Russian was once again promoted as the language of progress and internationalism.

This cultural crackdown was merely the prelude to the physical annihilation that was to come. The Great Purge, the wave of state terror that convulsed the entire Soviet Union from 1936 to 1938, fell upon the BSSR with catastrophic force. The NKVD, the successor to the OGPU, arrested people by the tens of thousands based on quotas sent from Moscow. The targets were anyone deemed remotely unreliable: former members of non-Bolshevik parties, priests, Poles, peasants who had resisted collectivization, and, above all, the party and state elite itself. Almost the entire government of the BSSR was arrested and shot as "enemies of the people." Out of the 139 PhD students at the Belarusian Academy of Sciences in 1934, only six avoided arrest or execution.

The terror reached its symbolic and horrifying climax on the night of October 29-30, 1937. In the basement of the NKVD prison in Minsk, more than 100 of Belarus's most prominent cultural and intellectual figures were executed by firing squad. The victims included over twenty of the nation's leading writers and poets, men who had created modern Belarusian literature. This event, which became known as the "Night of the Executed Poets," effectively decapitated the nation's cultural elite. It was a blow from which Belarusian culture would not recover for generations. Across the republic, in places like the Kurapaty forest outside Minsk, the NKVD created killing fields, executing tens of thousands of ordinary citizens and burying them in unmarked mass graves.

By 1939, on the eve of another world war, the Byelorussian Soviet Socialist Republic had been transformed. The quiet, agrarian land of the early 1920s had become a place of new factories and sprawling collective farms. But this modernization had been achieved at a terrible price. The peasantry was subjugated, the intellectual class was liquidated, and society was atomized by fear. The national revival of the 1920s was a distant memory, its leaders and its literature either dead or banned. The BSSR was now a loyal and terrified component of Stalin's monolithic Soviet state, its people bracing for the next storm that was gathering on their western border.

CHAPTER FIFTEEN: The Great Patriotic War: Occupation and the Partisan Movement

For twenty months, the Byelorussian Soviet Socialist Republic, now swollen with its newly acquired western territories, existed in a state of uneasy peace, a nervous interlude between the trauma of internal repression and the gathering storm to the west. The pact that had allowed for the "reunification" of Belarus in 1939 was a cynical marriage of convenience between two totalitarian regimes, and its dissolution was as inevitable as it was violent. The storm broke just before dawn on June 22, 1941. Without a declaration of war, Nazi Germany launched Operation Barbarossa, a surprise invasion of the Soviet Union on a massive scale. For Belarus, positioned directly in the path of Army Group Centre, the most powerful of the three German army groups, this was not the beginning of a war; it was the beginning of the apocalypse.

The Soviet defenses, caught completely off guard by a combination of Stalin's disbelief in intelligence warnings and the decapitation of the Red Army's officer corps during the purges, collapsed almost immediately. German Panzer divisions sliced through the frontline units, their *Luftwaffe* bombers destroying Soviet aircraft on the ground. The initial hours of the war were a scene of chaos and slaughter. One of the few places where a concerted defense was mounted was at the Brest Fortress, on the new border. Here, a small garrison, cut off and surrounded, fought with desperate courage for weeks against overwhelming odds, a stand that would become one of the foundational legends of the war.

Elsewhere, the Soviet Western Front disintegrated. In the first week of the war, German panzers executed a vast pincer movement, closing a trap around Soviet forces in a huge pocket between Białystok and Minsk. Hundreds of thousands of Red Army soldiers were killed or captured. On June 28, just six days into the invasion, Minsk fell to the Wehrmacht. The speed of the German advance was breathtaking. By the end of August 1941, all of Belarus was under German occupation. The initial phase of the war had been one of the most catastrophic defeats in military history.

The German occupation brought with it a "New Order" rooted in a savage racial ideology. According to Nazi plans, the Slavs were *Untermenschen*, or subhumans, destined for enslavement or extermination to create *Lebensraum*, or living space, for German colonists. The territory of Belarus was carved up. The eastern areas remained under military administration as the rear of Army Group Centre, a southern slice was attached to *Reichskommissariat* Ukraine, and a district around Białystok was annexed directly to East Prussia. The core of the country was organized into the *Generalbezirk Weißruthenien*, a subdivision of the vast *Reichskommissariat Ostland*.

For the people of Belarus, this new administrative map meant little. The reality of occupation was a regime of terror and systematic plunder. Food, livestock, and industrial equipment were ruthlessly expropriated for the German war effort. Civilians were rounded up and shipped to Germany as *Ostarbeiter*, slave laborers, to work in factories and on farms. The brutality of the occupation was intended to cow the population into submission, but it would ultimately have the opposite effect.

The most horrific dimension of the New Order was the Holocaust. Belarus had been a heartland of Jewish life for centuries, and its Jewish population had swelled with refugees from Poland after 1939. For the Nazis, this was a land to be cleansed. The work of extermination began immediately. Mobile killing squads, the *Einsatzgruppen*, followed in the wake of the army, rounding up Jewish men, women, and children. In cities like Minsk, Vitebsk, and Gomel, ghettos were established, fenced-off areas where the Jewish population was concentrated in conditions of appalling starvation and disease. These ghettos were not intended as long-term settlements, but as holding pens for mass murder.

The killings were carried out with industrial efficiency and unimaginable cruelty. The primary method was shooting. Victims were marched to pits in nearby forests, forced to undress, and machine-gunned. One of the largest such killing sites in the occupied Soviet Union was Maly Trostenets, on the outskirts of Minsk. Here, Jews from the Minsk ghetto, along with tens of thousands of Jews deported by train from Germany, Austria, and Czechoslovakia, were systematically murdered. Later, mobile gas vans were also used. By the end of the occupation, it is estimated that between 500,000 and 800,000 Belarusian Jews had been murdered, a near-total annihilation of a community that had been an integral part of the country's fabric for six hundred years.

In the face of this terror, resistance began to stir. The first partisans were Red Army soldiers who had escaped the great encirclements of the summer of 1941, hiding in the vast forests and swamps that covered nearly a third of the republic. Initially, these groups were small, isolated, and poorly equipped, fighting for their own survival. However, as German brutality intensified, their ranks swelled with local villagers seeking revenge or simply a way to fight back.

By 1942, Moscow had recognized the strategic potential of this burgeoning guerrilla movement. A Central Staff of the Partisan Movement was established under the command of Panteleimon Ponomarenko, the pre-war head of the Belarusian Communist Party, to coordinate and supply the scattered detachments. Radio operators, commanders, and demolition experts were parachuted in from the "mainland." The movement was transformed from a spontaneous reaction into an organized and centrally directed second front, a vital component of the Soviet war effort. Belarus, with its dense forests and impassable marshes, became the epicenter of the Soviet partisan war. At its peak, the movement comprised nearly 375,000 fighters, supported by a vast network of underground activists in the towns and villages.

The partisans' primary mission was to disrupt the German war machine. Their main target was the railway network that supplied Army Group Centre. In a series of massive, coordinated operations known as the "rail war," tens of thousands of partisans descended on the tracks at night, blowing up rails, derailing trains, and destroying bridges. They ambushed German convoys, attacked isolated garrisons, and gathered crucial intelligence. By 1943, large swathes of the countryside had become "partisan zones," areas where German authority had effectively collapsed and Soviet power had been re-established deep behind enemy lines. In some of these zones, partisans even sowed and harvested crops on collective farms to feed themselves and the local population.

The Germans responded to the partisan threat with a policy of collective terror. Their anti-partisan operations, euphemistically termed *Bandenbekämpfung* ("bandit fighting"), were wars against the entire civilian population. The strategy was to create a desert, to drain the "swamp" in which the partisan "fish" swam. Entire villages suspected of aiding the partisans were surrounded, their inhabitants either shot or herded into barns and burned alive. At least 5,295 Belarusian settlements were destroyed in such punitive actions.

The most infamous of these massacres occurred on March 22, 1943, in the village of Khatyn. In retaliation for a partisan ambush that killed a German officer, troops from a collaborationist auxiliary police battalion, assisted by an SS special unit, descended on the village. They rounded up all 149 residents, including 75 children, forced them into a large wooden shed, set it on fire, and shot anyone who tried to escape the flames. The village of Khatyn was wiped from the face of the earth, its fate becoming a powerful and horrifying symbol of the suffering of the Belarusian people during the war.

While the majority of the population resisted the occupiers, some chose the path of collaboration. Motivations varied. Some were simply opportunists; others were anti-communists who saw the Germans as liberators from Stalin's terror. A small number of nationalist leaders, hoping to use the war to achieve an independent state, agreed to work with the occupiers. The Germans, with little enthusiasm, permitted the creation of a limited form of local self-government, culminating in the establishment of the Belarusian Central Council (*Rada*) in late 1943, a body with no real power. They also formed local auxiliary police battalions (*Schutzmannschaften*) which were often used in the brutal work of the Holocaust and anti-partisan operations.

The war also saw conflicts between different resistance groups. In Western Belarus, the Polish Home Army (*Armia Krajowa*) was active, fighting for a restored Poland that would include the territories lost in 1939. Its relationship with the Soviet partisans was deeply hostile, often escalating into open combat. For Jewish partisans, such as the famous Bielski group who created a family camp that saved over 1,200 people, survival meant navigating the dangers posed not only by the Germans but also by the antisemitism present in some Polish and even Soviet detachments.

The liberation of Belarus began in the autumn of 1943, as the Red Army, having turned the tide of the war at Stalingrad and Kursk, began to push westward, freeing the first towns in the east of the republic. The final act came in the summer of 1944. On June 22, the third anniversary of the invasion, the Soviet Union launched Operation Bagration, a colossal offensive designed to smash Army Group Centre and clear the path to Berlin.

The scale of the operation was immense. Over two million Soviet soldiers, supported by thousands of tanks and aircraft, fell upon the German lines. The partisan brigades played a crucial role, launching a massive wave of sabotage attacks in the days before the offensive, paralyzing the German rear and sowing chaos. The German front, stretched thin and with its reserves diverted to Normandy, shattered. In a repeat of 1941, but in reverse, vast German forces were encircled and annihilated. On July 3, 1944, Red Army tank crews, after fierce street fighting, liberated the ruins of Minsk. By the end of August, all of Belarus was free.

The land that was liberated was a wasteland. The three years of occupation had inflicted a demographic catastrophe unparalleled in modern European history. It is estimated that Belarus lost between a quarter and a third of its pre-war population. More than 200 towns and 9,000 villages had been destroyed. Minsk was over 80 percent rubble. The economy was non-existent. The republic that had been caught in the crossfire of the twentieth century's most brutal war had survived, but it was a land of ghosts, its landscape scarred by mass graves and the chimneys of burned-out villages.

CHAPTER SIXTEEN: Post-War Reconstruction and Sovietization

When the last German soldier was driven from Belarusian soil in the late summer of 1944, the Red Army liberated not a country, but a charnel house. Three years of Nazi occupation and the relentless partisan war had left behind a landscape of almost unimaginable ruin. This was the land the Germans had designated for *Lebensraum*, a territory to be cleansed of its "subhuman" population to make way for colonists. Their failure to win the war did not prevent them from coming terrifyingly close to achieving that demographic goal. An estimated quarter of the republic's population had perished. The demographic loss was so profound that the Byelorussian SSR would only return to its pre-war population level in 1971.

The material destruction was just as staggering. More than 200 towns and 9,000 villages had been systematically destroyed. The major cities of Minsk and Vitebsk were over 80 percent rubble, their infrastructure nonexistent. The republic's industrial base, modest as it had been, was completely wiped out, its factories either dismantled and shipped to Germany or simply dynamited during the retreat. What remained of the rural economy was a smattering of emaciated livestock and fallow fields littered with the debris of war. The Byelorussian Soviet Socialist Republic in 1944 was a republic of ghosts and ruins, facing a future that had to be built, quite literally, from the ground up.

The task of reconstruction began before the war in Europe had even ended. As the front moved west, teams of sappers, construction workers, and party officials followed in the wake of the army. The immediate priorities were to restore basic services—railways, roads, electricity—and to get the population through the coming winter. The labor force was a cross-section of the survivors: women, teenagers, and elderly men, who formed the backbone of the workforce, supplemented by Red Army soldiers and, in a turn of historical irony, tens of thousands of German prisoners of war. They cleared rubble by hand, lived in dugouts and makeshift shelters, and worked with a grim determination born of exhaustion and the simple need to survive.

The centerpiece of this colossal effort was the rebuilding of Minsk. The pre-war city, with its labyrinth of old streets and diverse architecture, had been almost entirely erased. Soviet planners, arriving from Moscow, saw not a tragedy but a blank slate. The decision was made not to reconstruct the old city, but to build a new one, a showcase of Stalinist urban design. The new Minsk would be a city of grand ensembles, broad avenues, and monumental squares. A new central artery, Stalinski Prospekt (later Leninski Prospekt, and today's Independence Avenue), was carved through the ruins, lined with imposing neo-classical buildings meant to project an image of order, power, and permanence. This was not just rebuilding; it was a profound act of ideological re-inscription, transforming the capital into a model socialist city.

While the citizens of Minsk cleared rubble, the Kremlin was busy securing the republic's political future. As the war drew to a close, Stalin settled his accounts. In August 1945, a new border treaty was signed with the Soviet-controlled government of Poland. This agreement largely confirmed the line established by the Molotov-Ribbentrop Pact in 1939. The BSSR retained most of the western territories it had annexed, but the Białystok region and some other areas were returned to Poland. This finalization of the border was accompanied by a brutal series of population exchanges. Hundreds of thousands of ethnic Poles still living in the BSSR were expelled westward, while Belarusians in Poland were moved east, an effort to create ethnically homogenous states and eliminate the cross-border minorities that had complicated the politics of the region for centuries.

Simultaneously, the NKVD moved to re-establish absolute control. The return of Soviet power was accompanied by a new wave of purges. Anyone who had served in German-created local administrations or police units was arrested, as were former prisoners of war and slave laborers returning from Germany, who were automatically suspected of being "ideologically contaminated." The security organs also launched a ruthless campaign to liquidate the last pockets of armed resistance, particularly the Polish Home Army and the anti-Soviet "forest brothers" who continued to wage a guerrilla struggle against the new regime, especially in the newly-annexed western regions. By the late 1940s, this resistance had been crushed.

In a surprising and canny diplomatic move, Stalin leveraged the BSSR's immense suffering to gain a greater voice for the Soviet Union on the world stage. At the Yalta Conference, he insisted that, in recognition of their contribution to the victory, both the Ukrainian and Byelorussian SSRs should be granted their own seats at the newly formed United Nations. The Western allies, though skeptical, eventually agreed. Thus, on October 24, 1945, the Byelorussian Soviet Socialist Republic became a founding member of the UN, complete with its own vote in the General Assembly. It was a purely symbolic sovereignty; the BSSR's delegation was staffed by loyal communists who voted in perfect lockstep with the main Soviet delegation. Nonetheless, it gave the republic a flag and a nameplate in New York, a strange quirk of Cold War politics.

With the republic's borders secured and its political landscape cleansed of opposition, the authorities turned to forging a new official identity for the BSSR. The central, foundational myth became the heroic struggle of the Great Patriotic War. Belarus was officially christened the "Partisan Republic." This powerful narrative cast the entire population as heroic anti-fascist fighters, led, of course, by the Communist Party. The partisan war was enshrined as the republic's defining experience, a trial by fire that had earned it a place of honor within the Soviet family of nations. This myth was heavily promoted in books, films, and monuments, becoming the unquestionable core of Soviet Belarusian patriotism.

This ideology was embodied by the republic's post-war leadership. An entire generation of former partisan commanders was promoted to positions of power, forming a new political elite whose legitimacy was rooted in their wartime credentials. The ultimate example of this trajectory was Pyotr Masherov, a former teacher who had become a legendary partisan leader and Hero of the Soviet Union. After holding various party posts, Masherov would become First Secretary of the Communist Party of Byelorussia in 1965, ruling the republic for fifteen years as a deeply popular and respected leader who was seen as the personification of the Partisan Republic.

Underneath this heroic narrative, the pre-war projects of industrialization and Sovietization resumed with an even greater intensity. The post-war Five-Year Plans transformed the BSSR into a major industrial hub, the "assembly shop of the Soviet Union." Moscow prioritized the development of heavy industry, machine-building, and chemicals. On the ruins of a pre-war aircraft facility, the Minsk Tractor Works (MTZ) was established by a decree in May 1946. In 1953, it rolled out its first signature wheeled tractor, the "Belarus," a model that would become one of the Soviet Union's most successful exports and a ubiquitous symbol of the republic's industrial prowess. It was soon joined by the Minsk Automobile Plant (MAZ), which produced heavy-duty trucks, and a host of other enterprises specializing in everything from refrigerators to high-tech electronics and computers. This rapid industrialization fueled massive urbanization, with Minsk in particular growing at a breakneck pace.

This industrial boom was accompanied by a renewed and intensified program of Russification. While the Belarusian language remained one of two official languages, Russian was the undisputed language of power, progress, and prestige. The party apparatus, the officer corps, technical manuals for the new factories, and higher education were all dominated by Russian. An influx of Russian managers, engineers, and party officials to oversee the reconstruction further cemented the language's dominance in the cities. Minsk, rebuilt as a Soviet metropolis, became a largely Russian-speaking city. This process was openly encouraged by the state. In 1959, Soviet leader Nikita Khrushchev declared in a speech in Minsk, "The sooner we all start speaking Russian, the faster we shall build communism." For many

Belarusians, fluency in Russian became a simple prerequisite for social and economic advancement.

In the countryside, particularly in the western regions that had been part of Poland before 1939, the state launched its final assault on the traditional way of life. Having been spared the collectivization campaigns of the 1930s, these regions were now subjected to the same brutal process. Peasants were forced to give up their private plots and join the *kolkhozes*. Resistance, though widespread, was met with arrests and deportations. By the early 1950s, the collectivization of the entire republic was complete, establishing total state control over agriculture.

The death of Stalin in 1953 brought a palpable sense of relief. The "Thaw" under Khrushchev saw an end to mass terror, the release of some political prisoners from the Gulag, and a marginal increase in cultural expression. Life remained hard, but the constant, paralyzing fear of the midnight knock on the door receded. For the next few decades, the Byelorussian Soviet Socialist Republic settled into a predictable rhythm. It became, in many ways, a model Soviet republic. Its industry was productive, its agriculture was relatively efficient by Soviet standards, and its population was seen as reliably loyal and "Sovietized." Having risen from the ashes of total war, it was a land defined by its sprawling factories, its vast collective farms, and the omnipresent, carefully curated memory of the partisan struggle, a stable and seemingly permanent fixture on the western edge of the Soviet empire.

CHAPTER SEVENTEEN: The Chernobyl Disaster and its Lingering Shadow

In the spring of 1986, the Byelorussian Soviet Socialist Republic was the picture of mature socialism. Under the steady, if uninspired, leadership of Nikolai Slyunkov, it was a land of quiet predictability. The grand avenues of Minsk, rebuilt from rubble into a model Soviet city, hummed with the traffic of MAZ trucks and the quiet pride of a republic known as the USSR's "assembly shop." In the sprawling collective farms, the annual cycle of planting and harvesting unfolded with a familiar rhythm. The trauma of the Great Patriotic War, though enshrined in countless memorials, was a generation in the past. The terror of the Stalinist purges was a topic best left unspoken. For most of its ten million citizens, life in the BSSR was stable, orderly, and seemingly permanent. The new winds of *glasnost* and *perestroika*, just beginning to blow from Mikhail Gorbachev's Moscow, were still little more than a distant rumor.

Just across the southern border, deep in the marshy woodlands of Ukrainian Polesia, stood the Vladimir Ilyich Lenin Nuclear Power Plant, better known by the name of the nearby town, Chernobyl. It was a flagship of Soviet technological prowess, one of the largest nuclear power stations in the world. Its four colossal RBMK-1000 reactors were a source of immense pride, potent symbols of the peaceful atom put to work for the glory of communism. For the people of southern Belarus, the plant was a familiar neighbor, a source of jobs for some and a distant, unremarkable feature of the landscape for most. It was simply part of the modern world, a testament to the power of Soviet science to tame the elements.

This faith in the absolute mastery of technology was about to be shattered. In the early hours of Saturday, April 26, 1986, the night shift in the control room of Chernobyl's Reactor No. 4 was running a safety test. The test, ironically designed to simulate a station blackout, was poorly planned and conducted in violation of numerous safety protocols. The operators, working with a reactor design that had a critical, undisclosed flaw—a tendency to surge with power under certain low-power conditions—found themselves in a situation they could not control. At 1:23 AM, they initiated an emergency shutdown. Instead of inserting the control rods and dampening the reaction, the flawed design caused a massive, instantaneous power spike.

What followed was a pair of titanic explosions. The first, a steam explosion, tore through the reactor. The second, a few seconds later, was a hydrogen explosion that blew the 2,000-ton concrete and steel lid, known as the "upper biological shield," clean off the reactor core. The containment building was ripped open to the night sky. A colossal column of fire, laced with incandescent fragments of uranium fuel and superheated graphite moderator, erupted from the gaping wound, rising a kilometer into the atmosphere. The heart of the atom, which Soviet science had claimed to tame, had broken its chains with unimaginable violence. Reactor No. 4 of the Chernobyl Nuclear Power Plant had ceased to exist.

The first to confront the inferno were the plant's own firefighters, who arrived on the scene within minutes, completely unaware of the lethal reality of what they were facing. They saw a fire, and their job was to put it out. Clad in simple canvas uniforms, they climbed onto the blazing, rubble-strewn roofs of the turbine hall, kicking aside chunks of radioactive graphite with their boots. They fought the flames with water, a futile gesture against a nuclear blaze that was melting metal, but their courage prevented the fire from spreading to the adjacent Reactor No. 3, an act that almost certainly averted an even greater catastrophe. Within hours, they began to fall, overcome by what they thought was the heat, their bodies assaulted by doses of radiation so immense they were effectively being cooked from the inside out. Twenty-eight of these first responders would die agonizing deaths from acute radiation sickness in the weeks that followed.

While these men were sacrificing their lives, the Soviet state reacted with its most deeply ingrained instinct: secrecy. The first reports that reached Moscow were confusing and downplayed the scale of the event. The instinct of the vast party bureaucracy was to contain not the radiation, but the information. Local officials sealed off the nearby city of Pripyat, but told its 50,000 residents nothing, advising them only to stay indoors. For the wider Soviet public, and for the world, there was only silence. The official news agency, TASS, remained mute.

The radioactive plume, meanwhile, was drifting on the wind. Rich with highly radioactive isotopes like iodine-131, caesium-137, and strontium-90, the cloud was invisible, tasteless, and odorless. Prevailing winds in the first crucial days after the explosion blew the most concentrated and dangerous parts of this toxic cocktail not east toward Russia or south toward Kyiv, but directly north and northwest, into the Byelorussian SSR. The heaviest fallout descended upon the lush fields, dense forests, and quiet villages of the Gomel and Mogilev regions. As the radioactive particles settled, an invisible poison began to work its way into the soil, the water, the plants, and the bodies of every living thing.

While the people of southern Belarus went about their weekend, completely oblivious to the danger raining down on them, the first alarm was sounded over 1,000 kilometers away. On the morning of Monday, April 28, workers arriving at the Forsmark Nuclear Power Plant in Sweden began setting off radiation alarms. Puzzled, the plant's operators checked for a leak, but found nothing. They soon realized the radiation was coming from outside. By tracing wind patterns, they pinpointed the source: somewhere in the western Soviet Union. Only then, confronted with irrefutable evidence from the outside world, did the Kremlin finally break its silence. That evening, on the main television news program *Vremya*, an announcer read a terse, 20-second statement acknowledging a minor accident at the Chernobyl plant.

Even with the admission, the full scale of the disaster was hidden. While the world watched in horror as the story slowly emerged, life in the BSSR was ordered to proceed as normal. The most grotesque example of this official denial came on May 1, the great socialist holiday of International Workers' Day. In Minsk, Gomel, and other Belarusian cities, just as in Kyiv, the traditional May

Day parades went ahead. Tens of thousands of people, including columns of schoolchildren in their Young Pioneer uniforms, marched through the streets, waving flags and flowers, breathing in air contaminated with radioactive iodine. The party leadership, aware of the radiation but terrified of causing a panic or displeasing Moscow, stood atop their reviewing stands, smiling and waving at the crowds.

The belated process of evacuation began, but it was slow and chaotic. The residents of the 30-kilometer zone around the plant in Ukraine were the first to be moved. In Belarus, however, where the contamination was in some areas even heavier, the response was tragically sluggish. It took days, and in some villages weeks, before the order came to leave. When it did, it was with a brutal finality. Residents were told they were leaving for three days and to take only essential documents and a change of clothes. They were forced to abandon everything: their homes, their furniture, their photographs, and their pets. They would never return. In the end, over 135,000 people were permanently evacuated from the most contaminated zones of Belarus. A new and chilling vocabulary entered the Belarusian language: words like "resettlement," "zone," and "radiation."

To contain the still-burning reactor and clean up the worst of the fallout, the Soviet state mounted a response on a military scale. A vast mobilization of personnel, known as the "liquidators," was dispatched to the disaster zone. Over 600,000 soldiers, reservists, miners, engineers, and scientists from across the USSR were thrown into the breach. A significant portion of these, around 100,000, came from Belarus. These men performed acts of incredible heroism in an environment of unprecedented danger. Miners dug a tunnel beneath the reactor to install a cooling system. Helicopter pilots flew daring sorties through the radioactive plume to drop tons of sand, boron, and lead onto the exposed core. On the ground, soldiers in hastily devised protective gear scrubbed down buildings and scraped up topsoil. The most famous were the "biorobots," soldiers who, after mechanical robots failed in the intense radiation fields, were sent onto the roof of the reactor building to clear away the deadly chunks of graphite by hand, allowed to work for only seconds at a time before being replaced. For their service, the liquidators received a small medal and, for many, a lifetime of radiation-induced illnesses.

The long-term consequences of this invisible poison soon began to manifest. The first and most undeniable health impact was a dramatic epidemic of thyroid cancer among children. Radioactive iodine-131, which had blanketed the region, was absorbed by pasture grass, eaten by cows, and concentrated in their milk. Children, whose thyroid glands are particularly active and who were encouraged to drink plenty of milk, received massive internal doses. In the years following the disaster, rates of pediatric thyroid cancer in the Gomel region skyrocketed to levels more than a hundred times the pre-Chernobyl average.

The broader health consequences remain a subject of intense scientific and political debate, but for the people living in the contaminated territories, the reality was a litany of new ailments. Rates of other cancers, leukemia, cardiovascular disease, and cataracts all saw increases. A generation of children was born with weakened immune systems and a host of chronic illnesses. Beyond the physically measurable effects was a pervasive and crippling psychological trauma. The constant fear of the unseen enemy in the food, the water, and the air created a condition of chronic stress and anxiety, a fatalistic mindset that became known as "Chernobyl syndrome."

The economic cost to the republic was staggering. The disaster effectively removed nearly a quarter of Belarus's forests and more than one-fifth of its agricultural land from production. The direct costs of evacuating and resettling communities, building new housing, and providing lifelong healthcare and social benefits to the affected population placed a crushing and permanent burden on the state budget. A vast, eerie wilderness was formally created in the most heavily contaminated area along the Ukrainian border: the Polesie State Radioecological Reserve. Covering over 2,000 square kilometers, it is a land returned to nature, an unintentional wildlife sanctuary where wolves, bison, and Przewalski's horses roam among the abandoned villages, a landscape forever haunted by the atom.

For the Byelorussian Soviet Socialist Republic, Chernobyl was more than a public health crisis or an environmental catastrophe. It was a political and psychological earthquake that cracked the very foundations of the Soviet system. The initial cover-up, the lies broadcast on television while radioactive clouds drifted overhead, and the perceived indifference and incompetence of the authorities in Moscow shattered the carefully constructed image of an omniscient and benevolent state. A deep sense of betrayal took root. The feeling grew that Belarus, a small republic that had no nuclear power plants of its own, had been sacrificed to protect the interests of the larger empire.

This anger and disillusionment fueled a powerful national awakening. The disaster gave the small, suppressed circle of the Belarusian intelligentsia a cause that was impossible to ignore and dangerous to silence. Writers like Ales Adamovich and Vasil Bykau used their moral authority to break through the wall of official silence, speaking out about the true scale of the suffering. A grassroots environmental and anti-nuclear movement began to form, which quickly morphed into a broader movement for national rights and political change. The Chernobyl disaster had poisoned the soil, but it had also fertilized the seeds of independence. The invisible fallout from Reactor No. 4 would radiate through the political landscape for years to come, its lingering shadow falling upon a system already beginning to crumble.

CHAPTER EIGHTEEN: The Path to Independence: The Late Soviet Period

To the casual observer in the mid-1980s, the Byelorussian Soviet Socialist Republic appeared as the very model of a successful Soviet republic. It was stable, productive, and seemingly content in its role as the westernmost bastion of the USSR. Its people, heavily Russified and governed by a conservative and deeply entrenched Communist Party apparatus, were considered among the most loyal of Soviet citizens. Yet beneath this placid surface, two seismic events were conspiring to fracture the foundations of the Soviet order. The first was the radioactive fallout from Chernobyl, which poisoned the land and shattered the people's trust in Moscow. The second was the arrival of Mikhail Gorbachev's policies of *glasnost* (openness) and *perestroika* (restructuring), which, however cautiously implemented in Minsk, created the first cracks in the monolith of state control.

The Communist Party leadership in Belarus greeted Gorbachev's reforms with a conspicuous lack of enthusiasm. They were products of the Brezhnev-era "period of stagnation," comfortable in their positions and deeply suspicious of any change that might disturb the carefully managed order. While newspapers in Moscow were beginning to publish daring critiques of the Soviet past, the press in Minsk remained timid. But the new atmosphere could not be contained by the republic's borders. The new openness allowed for the emergence of "informal" groups and associations, organizations that operated outside the rigid control of the Party.

Initially, these groups prudently avoided direct political challenges, focusing instead on culture and heritage. One of the most prominent was *Talaka*, a name invoking the traditional Belarusian custom of communal work. Formed by young intellectuals and students, *Talaka* dedicated itself to the preservation of historical monuments, the cleanup of polluted rivers, and the revival of folk traditions and holidays. They were, on the surface, harmless conservationists. In the context of Soviet

Belarus, however, this work was quietly revolutionary. By restoring a dilapidated church or celebrating an ancient folk rite, they were reasserting a history and an identity that was not centered on the October Revolution or the Great Patriotic War. They were gently reminding people of a past that was distinctly Belarusian.

This quiet cultural work was dramatically and horrifically superseded by the unearthing of a far more terrible past. In the spring of 1988, an archaeologist and art historian named Zianon Pazniak, along with his colleague Yauhen Shmyhalyou, began excavating a series of suspicious depressions in a pine forest on the northern outskirts of Minsk called Kurapaty. What they found were the skeletal remains of thousands upon thousands of people, piled in mass graves, each with a single bullet hole in the back of the skull.

On June 3, 1988, the weekly journal *Litaratura i mastatstva* ("Literature and Art") published a devastating article by Pazniak and Shmyhalyou titled "Kurapaty—The Road of Death". Based on their excavations and the testimonies of elderly villagers from the surrounding area, the article laid the blame for the massacre squarely on the Soviet secret police, the NKVD. They concluded that between 1937 and 1941, during the height of Stalin's Great Terror, this tranquil forest had been a killing field, an assembly line of death where the NKVD had systematically executed tens of thousands of Belarusian citizens.

The publication of the Kurapaty article was a bombshell that obliterated the foundational myth of the "Partisan Republic." The official narrative held that all suffering had come at the hands of foreign invaders, the Nazis. Kurapaty provided irrefutable proof that the Soviet state itself had been a merciless executioner of its own people. The revelation sent a shockwave of horror and anger through society. The government, after a clumsy attempt to blame the Nazis, was forced by public pressure to open an official investigation, which ultimately confirmed the NKVD's guilt. Kurapaty became Belarus's Katyn, a national wound and a powerful symbol of the crimes of the communist regime.

The raw emotion unleashed by the discovery found its political expression a few months later. Activists from *Talaka* and a new memorial society called "Martyrology of Belarus" called for a mass gathering to honor the victims on *Dziady*, the traditional Belarusian day for commemorating ancestors, on October 30, 1988. Thousands of people gathered in Minsk for what was intended to be a solemn procession to the execution site at Kurapaty. The authorities, panicked by the first large-scale unauthorized demonstration in decades, responded with brute force. The peaceful marchers were met by phalanxes of riot police, who attacked the crowd with water cannons and tear gas.

The violent dispersal of the *Dziady* demonstration was a profound political miscalculation. It radicalized the nascent movement, transforming a historical and moral grievance into an open political confrontation with the state. As the writer Vasil Bykau would later remark, on that day the people "went to Dziady as a population, and returned as a people."

The energy from Kurapaty and the crackdown at *Dziady* needed an organizational vessel. In October 1988, an organizing committee was formed to create a broad-based popular movement. This culminated in the founding congress of the Belarusian Popular Front "Rebirth" (BPF, or *Adradžennie*). Unable to meet in Minsk due to the authorities' refusal to grant permission, the 397 delegates convened across the border in Vilnius, the capital of Soviet Lithuania, in June 1989. They elected the man who had unearthed the Kurapaty graves, the fiery and uncompromising Zianon Pazniak, as their leader. The BPF's program was a direct challenge to the Soviet order: it called for genuine democracy, economic reform, a full accounting of the Chernobyl disaster, and, most importantly, the political and economic sovereignty of Belarus.

The late 1980s also saw a fierce public debate over the status of the Belarusian language. Decades of Russification had relegated it to the kitchen and the village, while Russian dominated every sphere of public life. Intellectuals, writers, and the new BPF activists launched a powerful campaign, gathering tens of thousands of signatures on petitions demanding that Belarusian be made the state language. The pressure was immense, and the Communist Party, beginning to lose its grip on the narrative, was forced to make concessions. In January 1990, the Supreme Soviet of the BSSR adopted a landmark Law on Languages. The law declared Belarusian the sole state language, while granting Russian the status of "language of interethnic communication." It laid out a gradual, ten-year transition period for government and education to switch over. For the national movement, it was a monumental victory.

The first test of the new political landscape came with the elections to the 12th Supreme Soviet in March 1990. The elections were far from free and fair; the Communist Party and its affiliated organizations still controlled the nomination process and the media. Nevertheless, it was the first time that genuine opposition candidates could compete. Despite the obstacles, the Belarusian Popular Front managed to run a spirited campaign. When the votes were counted, the communists and their allies had secured a huge majority. However, a small but determined opposition bloc of about thirty BPF deputies had won seats.

When the new parliament convened, this small faction, led by Pazniak, turned the staid, rubber-stamp legislature into a genuine political arena. Though hopelessly outnumbered, they were articulate, well-prepared, and relentless. They used the parliamentary rostrum, which was now being broadcast on television, to challenge the government, expose corruption, and relentlessly push the agenda of national sovereignty. Their presence shattered the illusion of monolithic unity that had defined Soviet politics for decades.

The push for sovereignty was gaining momentum across the Soviet Union. Inspired by the bold moves of the Baltic republics, the tide of "parade of sovereignties" was becoming unstoppable. The BPF opposition in the Supreme Soviet relentlessly pushed the issue, but the decisive factor was the changing calculus of the communist elite. Many party bosses, seeing the authority of the central government in Moscow crumbling, began to view republican sovereignty not as a threat, but as a potential lifeboat. It offered a way to preserve their own power by transforming themselves from Moscow's regional lieutenants into the rulers of their own domains.

On July 27, 1990, after intense debate, the Supreme Soviet of the Byelorussian SSR adopted the Declaration of State Sovereignty. The vote was nearly unanimous. The document proclaimed the "supremacy, independence, and plenitude of state power of the republic within the borders of its territory, the supremacy of its laws, [and] the independence of the republic in foreign relations." It was a pivotal moment, the first official step on the road out of the USSR. To be sure, it was not yet a declaration of full independence; Belarus was still a part of the Soviet Union, and the Communist Party was still in charge. But the declaration had fundamentally altered the relationship with Moscow. For the first time in centuries, a legislative body on Belarusian soil had asserted its right to be master in its own house. The path to full independence was now open, waiting only for the final collapse of the imperial center to be traversed.

CHAPTER NINETEEN: August 1991: The Declaration of a Sovereign State

The thirteen months that followed the Declaration of State Sovereignty in July 1990 were a period of profound and frustrating ambiguity for Belarus. The republic had a flag of sovereignty, but it still flew alongside the Soviet hammer and sickle. It had a law proclaiming the supremacy of its own constitution, but its economy, military, and security services remained umbilically linked to Moscow. It was a time of dual power, where the old Soviet structures, though visibly decaying, still held the levers of control, while the new democratic forces, though vocal and morally energized, lacked the parliamentary muscle to force a decisive break.

The political life of the republic was defined by a stalemate in its Supreme Soviet. On one side was the conservative communist majority, the nomenklatura who ran the collective farms, the factories, and the party committees. They were masters of procedure and inertia, adept at slowing down, diluting, or simply ignoring any reform that threatened their authority or the integrity of the Union. Their leader, the Chairman of the Supreme Soviet Mikalai Dziemianciej (Nikolai Dementei), embodied this cautious, apparatchik mindset.

On the other side was the small but ferocious opposition bloc of the Belarusian Popular Front. Led by the archaeologist-turned-politician Zianon Pazniak, the BPF deputies were hopelessly outnumbered but refused to be outmaneuvered. They used the parliamentary chamber as a stage for political theater, delivering impassioned speeches about national history, the crimes of communism revealed at Kurapaty, and the lingering tragedy of Chernobyl. While they rarely won a vote, their televised performances introduced new ideas into the public sphere and chipped away at the legitimacy of the old guard.

The general population, for its part, remained largely passive. Unlike in the neighboring Baltic states or Ukraine, there was no mass, grassroots movement for independence in Belarus. The April 1991 workers' strikes, which saw thousands take to the streets, were initially sparked by price hikes and only later took on political demands. A referendum held in March 1991 on the future of the USSR revealed the prevailing sentiment: 83 percent of Belarusians voted in favor of preserving the Soviet Union, albeit in a reformed state. The idea of a complete rupture with Moscow was, for many, simply unthinkable.

The catalyst for the final, sudden break would not come from Minsk, but from Moscow. On the morning of Monday, August 19, 1991, Soviet television channels broadcast a startling announcement. A group calling itself the State Committee on the State of Emergency (known by its Russian acronym, GKChP) had taken power. President Mikhail Gorbachev, they claimed, was ill at his dacha in the Crimea. The committee, composed of hardline communist officials including the Vice President, the KGB chief, and the Minister of Defense, declared a state of emergency, banned demonstrations, and sent tanks rolling into the streets of Moscow. Their goal was to halt the signing of a new Union Treaty that would have devolved significant power to the republics and, they believed, lead to the disintegration of the country.

The reaction from the leadership of the Byelorussian SSR was one of telling silence. As Boris Yeltsin, the president of the Russian Federation, climbed atop a tank outside the Russian White House in Moscow to defy the coup plotters, the Communist Party bosses in Minsk waited. They issued no condemnation of the unconstitutional seizure of power. Their behavior was widely interpreted as a quiet endorsement, a wait-and-see approach that sided with the hardliners should they succeed. For the old guard, the coup was a potential godsend, a chance to turn back the clock and crush the irritating democratic opposition for good.

The BPF and other democratic activists reacted with immediate defiance. Though they lacked the numbers to fill the streets as Muscovites had, they organized protests and worked furiously to distribute information and condemn the GKChP. The contrast was stark and absolute: the democratic opposition risked their freedom to stand against the coup, while the communist leadership sat on its hands, awaiting instructions from the new masters in the Kremlin.

But the new masters were proving to be remarkably inept. The August Coup was poorly organized and met with unexpectedly fierce resistance in Moscow. After three tense days, it collapsed. The plotters were arrested, and a triumphant Yeltsin, not Gorbachev, emerged as the undisputed center of power in a rapidly dissolving empire. For the communist leaders in Minsk, this was a disaster. Their tacit support for the failed coup had left them utterly discredited and politically vulnerable. They had gambled on the past, and the future had just run them over.

The Belarusian Popular Front saw its moment. The opposition deputies immediately demanded an emergency session of the Supreme Soviet to address the leadership's conduct during the coup. On August 24, the deputies convened in Minsk. Outside the parliament building, thousands of citizens, mobilized by the BPF, had gathered, their presence a powerful source of pressure on the nervous communists inside.

The atmosphere in the chamber was electric. The communist majority, which had ruled with impunity for decades, was suddenly on the defensive, leaderless and demoralized. The BPF deputies, once a marginal irritant, now held the moral and political high ground. Zianon Pazniak and his allies went on the offensive, relentlessly attacking the leadership for its complicity and cowardice. In a moment of high drama, BPF deputy Valiantsin Holubeu brought a large white-red-white flag—the historical national banner, which was not yet an official symbol—into the parliamentary chamber, a potent visual challenge to the Soviet red flag that still hung there.

Under this intense pressure, the old order crumbled with astonishing speed. The first casualty was Chairman Mikalai Dziemianciej, who was forced to resign in disgrace for his support of the coup. Then, seizing the political initiative, the opposition pushed forward a series of revolutionary proposals. The most important of these was a law to give the Declaration of State Sovereignty, passed a year earlier, the full and immediate status of constitutional law. This was no longer a statement of intent; this was a legal act of secession.

On August 25, 1991, the Supreme Soviet held the historic vote. Overwhelmed by the pressure from the streets, the collapse of their patrons in Moscow, and the aggressive tactics of the opposition, the communist deputies capitulated. A large majority voted in favor. With the passage of this law, the Byelorussian Soviet Socialist Republic legally became an independent state. The long journey that had begun with the quiet work of 19th-century poets and folklorists had culminated in a parliamentary vote, triggered by a failed coup 700 kilometers away.

The revolution continued. In the same session, the Supreme Soviet voted to temporarily suspend the activities of the Communist Party of Byelorussia, the institution that had held a monopoly on power for seventy years. Its vast property holdings were nationalized. The KGB was also brought under the control of the republican government.

The final piece of the immediate political puzzle was to find a new leader. The parliament needed a new chairman to guide it through the uncharted waters of independence. The choice fell upon Stanislav Shushkevich, a respected nuclear physicist who had gained public prominence for his work in exposing the truth about the Chernobyl disaster. Shushkevich was a compromise figure. As a corresponding member of the Academy of Sciences and a moderate, he was acceptable to the intelligentsia and the BPF. As a long-time, though not high-ranking, member of the Communist Party, he was not seen as a radical threat by the shaken but still numerous nomenklatura. On September 18, he was formally elected Chairman of the Supreme Soviet, effectively becoming the first head of state of a newly independent Belarus.

With a new leader in place, the Supreme Soviet moved to formalize the country's new identity. On September 19, 1991, a law was passed changing the official name of the state from the "Byelorussian Soviet Socialist Republic" to the "Republic of Belarus." On the same day, the new state symbols were officially adopted: the historical white-red-white flag and the ancient coat of arms, the Pahonia, featuring a charging knight on horseback. These symbols, rooted in the Grand Duchy of Lithuania and the short-lived 1918 republic, were a definitive visual break with the Soviet past and a reclamation of a deeper European history.

The whirlwind of events in late August and September 1991 had been breathtaking. In the space of a few weeks, a seemingly stable and conservative Soviet republic had been propelled into full independence. A new name, a new flag, and a new leader were in place. But the foundations of the new state were fragile. The independence had been achieved not by a popular mass movement, but by a confluence of events: the terminal decay of the imperial center and the political miscalculation of the local communist elite, expertly exploited by a small but determined parliamentary opposition. The old nomenklatura, though temporarily disgraced, had not disappeared; its members still ran the ministries, the factories, and the farms. They had lost a battle, but they had not yet lost the war for the future of the new state.

CHAPTER TWENTY: The Lukashenka Era: The Consolidation of Power

The independence that fell upon Belarus in the autumn of 1991 was less a triumphant victory and more a bewildering accident. The state had a new name, a new flag, and a new seat at the United Nations, but on the ground, little had changed. The same men who had run the collective farms and factory floors as loyal communists now ran them as the managers of a sovereign state. The economy, severed from the arteries of the vast Soviet organism, went into freefall. The early years of independence were a time of dizzying hyperinflation, where prices could double in a month and life savings vanished into thin air. For the average citizen, the new reality was not one of national rebirth but of shuttered factories, empty store shelves, and a gnawing uncertainty about the future.

This economic chaos was mirrored by political paralysis. The government was a fractured and contentious affair. The head of state, the quiet intellectual Stanislav Shushkevich, favored cautious, pro-Western reforms and a strengthening of Belarusian national identity. He found himself locked in a constant power struggle with the Prime Minister, Vyacheslav Kebich, a consummate Soviet-era apparatchik who represented the powerful industrial and agricultural lobby. Kebich and his allies, the old nomenklatura, had little interest in market reforms or national revival; their primary goal was to preserve their own power and restore the broken economic ties with Russia. The Supreme Soviet, the nation's parliament, was the stage for their endless quarrels, a place of high rhetoric and little action, while the country drifted rudderless.

Amidst this climate of disillusionment and decay, a new figure began to make his presence felt on the political scene. He was a man from the provinces, the director of a state farm, or *sovkhoz*, with a folksy, combative speaking style that stood in stark contrast to the stilted jargon of the Minsk elite. His name was Alexander

Lukashenka. A young deputy in the Supreme Soviet, he had made a name for himself as a populist crusader, a plain-speaking truth-teller who seemed to be the only person willing to confront the rampant corruption that was festering within the new establishment.

In 1993, Lukashenka was appointed to head a new parliamentary anti-corruption committee. He used the position with masterful skill, turning its hearings into a public spectacle. He delivered fiery, televised speeches, brandishing files and making explosive accusations against the highest officials in the land, including both Shushkevich and Kebich. Whether his claims were entirely accurate was almost beside the point; they resonated powerfully with a population that saw a new elite enriching itself while the country fell apart. He tapped into a deep well of nostalgia for the perceived order and stability of the Soviet past, casting himself as the outsider, the man of the people who would sweep the corrupt politicians out of Minsk and restore a sense of justice.

The opportunity to transform this populist anger into real power came with the adoption of a new constitution in March 1994. The document formally established a presidential republic, setting the stage for the country's first-ever presidential election. The establishment favorite was Prime Minister Kebich, who ran a campaign based on his experience and a promise of a monetary union with Russia. Shushkevich, who had been ousted from his position as Chairman of the Supreme Soviet over a minor corruption scandal involving a case of nails for his dacha, also ran, as did the nationalist leader of the Belarusian Popular Front, Zianon Pazniak.

Lukashenka entered the race as the ultimate underdog, his campaign a shoestring affair. His platform was simple and devastatingly effective: "return the republic to the people." He promised to crush corruption, halt the painful economic reforms, and rebuild the fraternal relationship with Russia. He presented himself not as a politician, but as a father of the nation, a strong hand to guide the country back from the abyss. To the surprise of the Minsk establishment, the message caught fire. In the first round of the election in June 1994, Lukashenka won a stunning 45% of the vote, with Kebich trailing far behind at 17%. In the second-round runoff in July, the result was a landslide. Alexander Lukashenka, the state farm director, was elected the first president of the Republic of Belarus with over 80% of the vote.

The new president wasted no time in demonstrating his intention to rule with a firm hand. He quickly found that the 1994 constitution, with its system of checks and balances, was an impediment to the swift and decisive action he had promised. The Supreme Soviet, though dominated by the same ex-communist nomenklatura he had railed against, was now an independent center of power, capable of blocking his decrees and questioning his policies. The president and the parliament were set on a collision course.

Lukashenka's solution was to bypass the parliament and appeal directly to the people. In the spring of 1995, he initiated a national referendum, placing four controversial questions before the electorate. The first asked to give the Russian language equal status with Belarusian, a direct challenge to the post-independence policy of Belarusianization. The second proposed replacing the historical white-red-white flag and Pahonia coat of arms with new state symbols that were a clear evocation of the emblems of the Byelorussian SSR. The third sought public approval for his policy of economic integration with Russia. The fourth and most crucial question asked for the power to dissolve the Supreme Soviet in the event of "systematic or gross violations of the constitution."

The referendum was a declaration of war on the nascent national identity and the existing political order. The parliamentary opposition, led by the BPF, was outraged. Nineteen of its deputies began a hunger strike inside the parliament building to protest what they saw as an unconstitutional power grab. In the dead of night, they were forcibly removed by masked security forces. The referendum went ahead on May 14, 1995. According to the official results, all four of the president's proposals were approved by overwhelming margins. A few days later, the white-red-white flag that had flown over the parliament building was ceremoniously taken down. The head of the presidential property administration, Ivan Titenkov, reportedly tore it into pieces. The Soviet-style red and green banner was raised in its place.

The 1995 referendum was a major victory for Lukashenka, but it did not resolve his fundamental conflict with the other branches of government. The Supreme Soviet continued to resist his authority, and the Constitutional Court, led by its chairman Valery Tsikhinya, began to rule against his decrees. By 1996, the political system had reached a state of open warfare. The parliament initiated impeachment proceedings against the president, accusing him of violating the constitution. Lukashenka, in turn, accused the parliament and the court of sabotaging his efforts to govern and announced his intention to hold another referendum, this time to adopt an entirely new constitution.

The proposed new constitution was a blueprint for an authoritarian super-presidency. It would extend the president's term in office from five to seven years, create a new, bicameral parliament, the lower house of which would be hand-picked, and give the president sweeping powers to appoint judges, the government, and the heads of the security services, all without parliamentary approval. It effectively eliminated the principle of the separation of powers, concentrating all meaningful authority in the hands of one man.

The constitutional crisis of 1996 drew international alarm. The Russian government, led by Prime Minister Viktor Chernomyrdin, flew to Minsk in a last-ditch effort to broker a compromise. A deal was signed in the middle of the night, in which Lukashenka agreed that the referendum results would be advisory, not binding, and the parliament agreed to halt its impeachment proceedings. But the ink was barely dry on the agreement before Lukashenka publicly reneged on the deal. He fired the head of the Central Election Commission, Viktar Hanchar, who had declared the referendum illegal, and replaced him with a loyalist.

The referendum was held on November 24, 1996. Unsurprisingly, the state-controlled media reported another landslide victory for the president. Lukashenka immediately declared the new constitution the law of the land. The 12th Supreme Soviet, the first and last freely elected parliament in the country's history, was dissolved. A new House of Representatives was formed, its members drawn from a list of deputies who had remained loyal to the president. The Constitutional Court judges were forced to resign or swear allegiance to the new order. The impeachment was dead, and with it, any semblance of democratic checks and balances.

With his political rivals in the legislature and judiciary neutralized, Lukashenka moved to consolidate his control over the entire state. He built what became known as the "vertical of power," a rigid, top-down system of administration in which the heads of all regional and local governments were no longer elected, but appointed directly by the president. This ensured that his commands were transmitted without question from his office in Minsk down to the smallest town and village.

The new system was cemented by a climate of fear. The late 1990s were marked by the sinister disappearances of several key opposition figures who might have posed a challenge to the president's authority. In 1999, Yury Zakharanka, the former Minister of Internal Affairs, and Viktar Hanchar, the defiant former head of the election commission, vanished without a trace, along with his associate, the businessman Anatol Krasouski. The following year, Dzmitry Zavadski, a television cameraman who had previously been Lukashenka's personal operator, also disappeared. Though the state denied any involvement, the disappearances sent a chilling message to anyone who dared to contemplate a serious challenge to the established order. By the dawn of the new millennium, the brief, chaotic, and hopeful experiment with post-Soviet democracy in Belarus was over. The Lukashenka era had begun in earnest, and the foundations of his power were now set in stone.

CHAPTER TWENTY-ONE: Navigating East and West: Foreign Policy in the New Millennium

With his power consolidated at home by the turn of the millennium, Alexander Lukashenka turned his attention to the complex and often perilous art of navigating Belarus's place in the world. For a country of its size and location, wedged between an expanding NATO and a resurgent Russia, this was never going to be a simple task. The foreign policy that emerged was a masterclass in strategic ambiguity, a political and economic balancing act designed to extract maximum benefits from all sides while surrendering ultimate control to none. Minsk's diplomacy in the new millennium became a cyclical drama of fraternal embraces with Moscow, cautious flirtations with Brussels and Washington, and periodic, family-style squabbles over the price of gas.

The undisputed cornerstone of this policy was the relationship with Russia. The two nations were bound by the 1999 Treaty on the Creation of a Union State, an ambitious document that envisioned a confederation with a common parliament, currency, and citizenship. For the Kremlin, the Union State was a vehicle for the peaceful, gradual reabsorption of its most loyal post-Soviet neighbor. For Lukashenka, it was a source of immense economic subsidies and a powerful symbol of Slavic brotherhood that resonated with his domestic base. He was a master at playing the role of Russia's staunchest ally, the dependable western outpost against an encroaching West.

This alliance, however, was less a romantic reunion and more a transactional marriage of convenience, prone to bitter disputes. The Belarusian economic model, a largely unreformed remnant of the Soviet system, was kept afloat by a steady IV drip of Russian support. Chief among these subsidies was the supply of crude oil and natural gas at heavily discounted, below-market prices. Belarus would import cheap Russian oil, refine it in its modernized

Soviet-era refineries, and then sell the resulting petroleum products to Europe at world market prices, pocketing the difference. It was an immensely profitable arrangement that formed the bedrock of the country's relative economic stability.

This dependency, however, gave Moscow enormous leverage, which it periodically used to pressure Minsk for greater integration. This dynamic gave rise to the recurring spectacle of the "gas wars" and "milk wars." In 2004, and more dramatically in 2007, the Russian state-owned gas giant Gazprom, citing Belarus's mounting debts, cut off supplies, forcing Minsk to agree to significant price hikes and to sell Gazprom a 50% stake in its national pipeline network, Beltransgaz. The 2007 dispute escalated when Russia also imposed an export duty on oil, and Minsk retaliated by siphoning oil from the Druzhba pipeline, which supplied Germany and Poland, causing a brief panic in European capitals. Similar disputes erupted over Belarusian exports of dairy and agricultural products to Russia, with Moscow's health inspectors periodically discovering mysterious contaminants in Belarusian milk or beef just as political tensions were rising.

Each of these spats followed a predictable pattern. Moscow would turn the economic screws. Lukashenka would respond with furious rhetoric, accusing the Kremlin of betrayal and of treating its closest ally with contempt. He would then pivot westward, hinting at a new openness to Europe and America. This strategy was dubbed the "multi-vector foreign policy," a term that described Minsk's attempts to counterbalance its overwhelming reliance on Russia by cultivating other relationships.

The relationship with the West was a mirror image of the one with Russia: a cycle of freeze and thaw. The United States and the European Union viewed Belarus as "the last dictatorship in Europe," and their policy was largely driven by concerns over human rights and the lack of democracy. After fraudulent elections and the suppression of opposition, the West would impose sanctions. In 2004, the United States passed the Belarus Democracy Act, authorizing support for civil society and media, and paving the way for targeted sanctions. The EU followed suit, imposing its own visa bans and asset freezes on officials deemed responsible for election fraud and repression, particularly after the harsh crackdowns that followed the 2006 and 2010 presidential elections.

These periods of frosty isolation would be followed by cautious thaws. Typically, when Lukashenka needed leverage against Moscow or sought to ease economic pressure, he would make a calculated conciliatory gesture, such as releasing a number of high-profile political prisoners. The West, eager to encourage any sign of liberalization, would respond by easing sanctions and re-engaging in dialogue. This cycle of repression-sanctions-release-thaw defined relations for much of the 2000s and 2010s.

A significant opportunity for rapprochement came in 2009 with the launch of the EU's Eastern Partnership (EaP) program, designed to deepen ties with six post-Soviet states. Belarus was invited to join, an offer it cautiously accepted. For Minsk, the EaP was a welcome tool to enhance its multi-vector policy, offering access to European funds and markets without the stringent political conditions of full membership. Belarus participated pragmatically, focusing on practical projects in trade, transport, and digital harmonization while resisting any moves that would be seen by Moscow as a definitive tilt toward the West.

Lukashenka's skill at navigating the treacherous currents between East and West was put to the test by two major geopolitical crises. The first was the Russo-Georgian War in August 2008. While the Kremlin expected its closest ally to immediately recognize the independence of the breakaway regions of South Ossetia and Abkhazia, Minsk equivocated. After an initial, "incomprehensible silence" that angered Moscow, Lukashenka offered verbal support for Russia's actions but pointedly refused to grant diplomatic recognition, a stance he would maintain despite years of Russian pressure.

A far greater challenge came in 2014 with Russia's annexation of Crimea and the subsequent war in Ukraine's Donbas region. For a country whose sovereignty Lukashenka had so fiercely, if selectively, defended, Russia's violation of Ukraine's borders was a deeply alarming precedent. He again performed a delicate balancing act. He declared that the annexation set a "bad precedent" but also noted that, "de facto," Crimea was now part of Russia. Belarus voted with Russia against a UN resolution condemning the annexation, but simultaneously refused to formally recognize the peninsula as Russian territory. Lukashenka skillfully used the crisis to reposition Belarus not as a Russian satellite, but as a neutral ground, a regional Switzerland. He stressed Belarus's interest in a stable and unified Ukraine and refused to allow Belarusian territory to be used as a staging ground for Russian aggression.

This posture paid significant diplomatic dividends. In September 2014, Minsk became the host for peace talks between Russia, Ukraine, and the OSCE. The resulting, though ultimately unsuccessful, agreements became known as the Minsk Protocol and Minsk II. Hosting the negotiations elevated Lukashenka's international stature, allowing him to play the role of a regional peacemaker and providing a compelling reason for the West to re-engage with him. This diplomatic opening, combined with the release of the last remaining political prisoners in 2015, led to the most significant thaw in relations with the West in two decades. In 2016, the European Union lifted most of its sanctions against Belarus, ushering in a period of pragmatic cooperation.

Alongside this east-west balancing act, Belarus actively sought to build relationships with powers further afield. The most important of these new partners was China. From early in his presidency, Lukashenka cultivated a close relationship with Beijing, admiring the Chinese model of state-controlled capitalism combined with firm political authority. This "iron brotherhood" evolved into a significant economic partnership. China provided billions of dollars in loans and investment, most notably for the flagship Great Stone Industrial Park near Minsk, a key hub in China's Belt and Road Initiative. The relationship offered Minsk a valuable alternative source of credit without the political conditions demanded by the West or the sovereignty concerns that came with Russian money. Belarus also nurtured idiosyncratic relationships with other states hostile to the West, most notably Hugo Chávez's Venezuela, engaging in oil-for-tractors swaps and joint ventures.

By the late 2010s, the multi-vector policy seemed to be paying off. Relations with the EU were the best they had ever been, the threat of US sanctions had receded, and the relationship with China was deepening. However, the foundational relationship with Moscow was becoming increasingly strained. The Kremlin, weary of subsidizing its recalcitrant ally, was pushing a "tax maneuver" in the oil industry that threatened to eliminate Belarus's main economic advantage. In exchange for continued economic support, Moscow was once again demanding "deeper integration" under the old Union State treaty, reviving talk of a common currency and supranational institutions. For Lukashenka, who had spent two decades expertly trading the rhetoric of integration for the reality of sovereignty, the price of Russian friendship was becoming uncomfortably high.

CHAPTER TWENTY-TWO: Society and Identity in Post-Soviet Belarus

To understand Belarusian society in the first two decades of the twenty-first century is to understand the terms of an unwritten, but widely understood, social contract. After the bewildering economic collapse and political chaos of the early 1990s, the new government of Alexander Lukashenka offered a simple, powerful bargain to its citizens. In exchange for political loyalty and a surrender of democratic participation, the state promised stability. This was not a promise of soaring wealth or Western-style consumerism, but something far more basic and, for many, more appealing: order, predictability, and a modest but guaranteed standard of living. It was a deal colloquially encapsulated in the earthy phrase, *charka i shkvarka*—a shot of vodka and a piece of fried pork fat. It meant a job for life, a pension at the end of it, and a government that would keep the wolves of privatization and geopolitical turmoil from the door.

The economic engine of this social contract was the "Belarusian model," a system that stood in stark defiance to the "shock therapy" that had roiled its neighbors. While Russia and Poland sold off state assets in a chaotic scramble of privatization, Belarus held fast to the commanding heights of its Soviet-era economy. The great industrial giants, like the Minsk Tractor Works (MTZ) and the Minsk Automobile Plant (MAZ), remained firmly in state hands, their workforces largely protected from the mass layoffs seen elsewhere. In the countryside, the collective farm, the *kolkhoz*, was not dismantled but preserved and subsidized, providing a social safety net and a familiar structure to rural life. This was not a dynamic or innovative economy, but for a generation scarred by the memory of hyperinflation, it was a dependable one, kept afloat by subsidized Russian energy and a guaranteed Russian market for its goods.

This state-managed economy fostered a unique social landscape. The cities, particularly the meticulously clean and orderly capital of Minsk, became showcases of this stability. Their wide, Soviet-era avenues were free of the jarring inequality visible in Moscow or Kyiv; there were few oligarchs and few beggars. Life was regimented and predictable. The state provided for its citizens from cradle to grave, with subsidized utilities, free healthcare, and a public education system that emphasized discipline and conformity. For many Belarusians, particularly the older generation, this was a fair trade. The anxieties of the modern world were held at bay in exchange for a quiet, if circumscribed, life.

Beneath this veneer of uniformity, however, lay a society deeply divided on the fundamental question of its own identity. The most visible fracture was the one that ran along linguistic lines. The brief, intense flourishing of the Belarusian language in the early 1990s was decisively reversed by the 1995 referendum, which elevated Russian to the status of a co-equal state language. In practice, this meant the overwhelming dominance of Russian in every sphere of public life. Government business, university lectures, television broadcasts, and the daily commerce of the cities were conducted almost exclusively in Russian. Minsk became a predominantly Russian-speaking capital.

The Belarusian language was not extinguished, but it was relegated to a niche. It became the language of the nationalist opposition, the urban intelligentsia, and a dwindling rural population. To speak Belarusian in the city was often to make a political statement, a conscious act of dissent against the prevailing cultural current. A small but vibrant ecosystem of Belarusian-language schools, publishing houses, and rock bands persisted, but they operated on the margins, a cultural archipelago in a Russophone sea. For many, the language question was a simple matter of pragmatism; Russian was the language of opportunity, the key to a career and a connection to a wider world.

This cultural dynamic was reinforced by the state's official interpretation of history. The government aggressively promoted a historical narrative that centered on one singular, defining event: the Great Patriotic War. The memory of the partisan struggle against the Nazis was elevated into a state religion, the foundational myth of the modern Belarusian state. This was not merely a matter of honoring the past; it was an active political project. The war narrative emphasized the shared sacrifice and fraternal bond between the Belarusian and Russian peoples, providing a historical justification for the close political alliance with Moscow.

Grandiose war memorials became the primary sites of national commemoration. The heroic defense of the Brest Fortress, the tragedy of the burned village of Khatyn, and the valor of the forest partisans were endlessly recounted in schools, museums, and state media. Other, more complex or inconvenient periods of Belarusian history were downplayed or ignored. The rich history of the Grand Duchy of Lithuania, with its European orientation and legal traditions, was treated with caution. The Belarusian People's Republic of 1918 was actively condemned as a brief, illegitimate experiment by bourgeois nationalists. The state's historical memory began in 1941, framing Belarusian identity not as a long, unique historical journey, but as that of a loyal, heroic junior partner in a larger Soviet and Russian story.

The Russian Orthodox Church, which enjoyed a dramatic revival after decades of Soviet suppression, became a key pillar of this official identity. The state gave the Church, which operates under the jurisdiction of the Moscow Patriarchate, a privileged position. Its black-domed churches were rebuilt and gilded, its leaders appeared at state functions, and its message of social conservatism and Slavic unity resonated with the government's own ideology. For many citizens, Orthodoxy became synonymous with being Belarusian or Russian, a shared spiritual bulwark against a perceived decadent and hostile West. In the western regions of the country, however, the Catholic Church remained a powerful force. With its historical ties to Poland and Lithuania, it represented a different civilizational pole, a quiet but persistent reminder of the country's multi-confessional and European past, often serving as a cultural haven for the Belarusian-speaking community.

For much of the 2000s, this carefully managed system of economic stability and ideological conformity seemed unshakable.

Yet, powerful forces of change were at work, largely beyond the state's control. A new generation was coming of age, one with no memory of the Soviet Union and no personal experience of the chaotic 1990s. They had grown up in an independent Belarus, and they took its existence for granted. Their aspirations were not defined by the simple promise of *charka i shkvarka*. They were connected to the world through a tool that would prove to be the single greatest challenge to the state's monopoly on information: the internet.

Unlike its neighbors Russia and China, Belarus for a long time pursued a relatively laissez-faire approach to regulating the internet. This created a burgeoning digital public square where alternative news, uncensored history, and sharp political satire could flourish, far from the drab conformity of state television. Social media platforms, particularly the Russian VKontakte and later the messaging app Telegram, became virtual spaces where a new generation could connect, debate, and form communities based on shared interests and values that had little to do with the official state ideology.

This digital revolution was supercharged by an unexpected economic success story. In 2005, the government, in a bid to diversify the economy, established the High-Tech Park (HTP), a special economic zone on the edge of Minsk that offered massive tax breaks to technology companies. The project was a stunning success, attracting foreign investment and sparking a domestic IT boom. Companies based in the HTP developed internationally renowned products, from the messaging app Viber to the online game *World of Tanks*. This created a new social class: a globally-oriented, well-educated, and often well-paid urban middle class of programmers, designers, and project managers.

These "IT-niki" were a world apart from the traditional proletariat of the tractor factories. They worked for international clients, traveled freely to Europe, and earned salaries in US dollars or Euros, insulating them from the fluctuations of the local economy. They were pragmatic, often apolitical, and had little interest in traditional nationalist rhetoric. Their values were shaped less by the partisan war and more by the meritocratic, libertarian culture of the global tech industry. Their quiet success demonstrated that it was possible to build a modern, European future in Belarus, a future that did not depend on state subsidies or nostalgia for the USSR.

As the 2010s progressed, a quiet, bottom-up cultural revival began to take hold, distinct from both the state's Soviet-centric narrative and the political nationalism of the opposition. It was a "soft Belarusianization," driven by culture and commerce rather than politics. Young designers began incorporating traditional folk patterns into modern fashion, making the *vyshyvanka*, the embroidered peasant shirt, a trendy symbol of national identity. Private businesses found that using the Belarusian language in their branding and advertising was a cool and effective way to stand out. Language courses, lectures on the history of the Grand Duchy, and guided tours of the country's castles became popular among the new urban middle class.

This was a new kind of patriotism. It was not overtly political or anti-Russian. It was a modern, confident, and often bilingual expression of a distinct Belarusian identity, comfortable with its European geography and its complex history. It was the identity of a generation that saw Belarus not as a "little sister" to Russia or a fortress against the West, but simply as their home, a normal European country with its own unique story.

By the end of the decade, the foundations of the old social contract were visibly fraying. The state-run economy, starved of Russian subsidies and resistant to reform, was stagnating. The promise of stability was beginning to look like a guarantee of stagnation. The generation that had accepted the bargain of *charka i shkvarka* was aging, while a new generation, digitally connected and culturally confident, had come of age with a different set of expectations. They had grown up with the symbols of sovereignty, and they were beginning to wonder what that sovereignty should feel like in practice. The old identity, rooted in the memory of a shared Soviet past, was being challenged by a new one, which looked to a future that was unapologetically its own. The quiet, orderly society that had defined the Lukashenka era was far more dynamic and divided than it appeared. It was a society pregnant with change, waiting for a spark to ignite it.

CHAPTER TWENTY-THREE: The 2020 Protests: A Nation Awakens

The year 2020 arrived in Belarus on a current of simmering discontent. The old social contract, the implicit promise of stability in exchange for political passivity, had been fraying for years. The state-run economy was stagnating, starved of the Russian subsidies that had long kept it afloat. A new, digitally-savvy generation had come of age, their aspirations and worldview shaped more by the global internet than by the monotone pronouncements of state television. The quiet, bottom-up revival of a modern, European Belarusian identity was bubbling just beneath the surface of the state's rigid Soviet nostalgia. The foundations of the system were brittle; all that was needed was a sufficient shock to crack them.

That shock came in the form of a global pandemic. As the COVID-19 virus swept across the world in the spring of 2020, governments everywhere locked down their societies and braced for a public health catastrophe. In Belarus, President Alexander Lukashenka responded with a theatrical display of contemptuous denial. He dismissed the global panic as a "psychosis," famously prescribing folk remedies such as drinking vodka, visiting the banya, and, most bizarrely, driving a tractor in the fields, declaring that "the tractor will heal everyone." While the rest of Europe was in lockdown, Belarus remained defiantly open. It was the only country on the continent where the professional football league continued to play, and on May 9th, Minsk held its traditional, large-scale Victory Day military parade, a spectacle of massed troops and elderly veterans that seemed reckless to many. This cavalier attitude, this visible detachment from the anxieties of his own people, created a profound sense of abandonment. As citizens organized their own volunteer networks to source protective equipment for doctors, a dangerous perception took hold: the state was not only out of touch, it was dangerously incompetent.

It was in this atmosphere of anxiety and disillusionment that the 2020 presidential election campaign began. Scheduled for August

9, the election was expected to be another carefully managed political ritual, a fifth re-election for the incumbent who had ruled for twenty-six years. The traditional political opposition, fractured and marginalized, was not expected to mount a serious challenge. But this time, something different happened. Three new figures, all from within the system, stepped forward, and in doing so, they captured the public imagination and transformed a scripted ceremony into a genuine political contest.

The first was Viktar Babaryka, the urbane and respected head of Belgazprombank, the Belarusian subsidiary of a major Russian bank. For two decades, he had been a quiet, successful manager and a noted patron of the arts. His candidacy represented competence, modernity, and a calm, managerial alternative to the president's increasingly erratic populism. His campaign struck a chord, and his team managed to collect a staggering 435,000 signatures in support of his nomination, a number that dwarfed the totals of all other candidates combined.

The second was Valery Tsapkala, a former ambassador to the United States and the founder of the wildly successful Minsk High-Tech Park. He represented the technocratic, globalized face of Belarus, the world of IT professionals who had flourished despite the state-run economy. His message was one of pragmatic reform and integration into the digital world economy.

The third, and perhaps most disruptive, was Siarhei Tsikhanouski, a charismatic YouTube blogger. His channel, "A Country for Life," featured raw, unvarnished interviews with ordinary people in the provincial towns and villages, documenting their frustrations with local corruption and economic stagnation. He traveled the country in his branded minivan, holding impromptu rallies that were part political protest, part public therapy session. He coined the defining slogan of the early campaign, a blunt and visceral metaphor for the country's long-serving leader: "Stop the cockroach!" His folksy, direct style resonated deeply with a population tired of the polished lies of the official media.

The state, accustomed to a pliant and predictable political landscape, reacted with alarm and brute force. On May 29, Siarhei Tsikhanouski was arrested in Hrodna during a signature-gathering picket, a move widely seen as a blatant political provocation. A few weeks later, on June 18, Viktar Babaryka and his son Eduard, his campaign manager, were also arrested on charges of financial crimes that appeared just as his popularity was cresting. In the end, the Central Election Commission refused to register the candidacies of both Babaryka and Tsapkala. The message was clear: no genuine challengers would be permitted.

It was a catastrophic miscalculation. The regime believed that by removing the figureheads, it had decapitated the protest movement. Instead, it had created three martyrs and set the stage for an unprecedented political improvisation. Denied the right to run himself, Siarhei Tsikhanouski had put forward his wife, Sviatlana Tsikhanouskaya, an English teacher and stay-at-home mother, as a stand-in candidate. After the arrest of her husband and the disqualification of the other leading men, she was suddenly thrust into the role of the main opposition candidate.

In a move of political brilliance, the campaigns of the three rejected male candidates united behind her. On July 16, Sviatlana Tsikhanouskaya appeared on stage flanked by two other women: Veranika Tsapkala, the wife of Valery, and Maria Kalesnikava, the professional flutist who had been Viktar Babaryka's campaign chief. This "female trio" became the instant and iconic symbol of the opposition. Their message was simple and powerful. Tsikhanouskaya made no claim to be a politician; she was running, she said, out of love for her husband and a desire to see all political prisoners freed. Her sole promise was that, if elected, she would hold a new, free, and fair election within six months, an election in which everyone, including the men who had been jailed, could participate.

This platform of unity and a return to basic fairness electrified the country. The trio embarked on a campaign tour that turned into a triumphant procession. In city after provincial city, they were greeted by enormous, festive crowds, numbers unheard of in the country's modern history. On July 30, in Minsk, they held a rally that drew an estimated 60,000 people, the largest opposition gathering since the country's independence. The imagery of the campaign was infectious. Kalesnikava would make a heart shape with her hands, Veranika Tsapkala would raise a V-for-victory sign, and Tsikhanouskaya would clench her fist. The three symbols became the universal gesture of the movement. For the first time, the people of Belarus could see, in plain sight, that they were not alone in their desire for change.

Election day, August 9, 2020, arrived in an atmosphere of tense anticipation. Voters, responding to opposition calls to show their numbers, formed long queues outside polling stations, many wearing white bracelets as a sign of solidarity. The authorities seemed to be bracing for a storm. In the afternoon, internet access across the country was almost completely shut down, a move designed to prevent protesters from coordinating and to stop independent observers from transmitting evidence of fraud.

That evening, the state-controlled media announced the results of an official exit poll: Alexander Lukashenka had won with just under 80% of the vote; Sviatlana Tsikhanouskaya had received less than 10%. For the tens of thousands who had flocked to her rallies and the millions who had quietly cast their ballots for her, the numbers were not just disappointing; they were a physical impossibility, a blatant and insulting fiction.

As dusk fell, the protests began. They erupted not just in Minsk, but in dozens of cities and towns across the country. They were spontaneous, leaderless, and furious. The state's response was immediate and savage. Columns of riot police (OMON) and internal troops descended on the crowds, deploying stun grenades, rubber bullets, and water cannons with a ferocity that shocked the nation. The night air was filled with the sound of explosions, sirens, and screams.

Over the next three nights, the country witnessed a level of state violence it had not seen since the Nazi occupation. The security forces engaged in what seemed like a punitive expedition against their own citizens. Thousands of people, many of them simply passers-by, were rounded up and herded into overcrowded detention centers. The most notorious of these was the Okrestina facility in Minsk. For days, the sounds of horrific beatings and tortured screams echoed from its walls. When the first detainees were released, they emerged into the daylight with their bodies covered in grotesque purple and black bruises, their faces swollen and deformed. They told terrifying, consistent stories of systematic torture: of being forced to lie on top of each other in cells, of being beaten with truncheons for hours, of being subjected to endless humiliation. The stories, photographs, and videos spread like wildfire on the Telegram messaging app, which had managed to circumvent the internet blockade. The regime's attempt to terrorize the population into submission had the opposite effect; it created a tidal wave of revulsion and rage.

The brutality of the state catalyzed a remarkable shift in the nature of the protest. On August 12, a new form of resistance appeared. Women, dressed in white and carrying flowers, began to form long, silent "chains of solidarity" along the main avenues of Minsk and other cities. It was a visually stunning and morally powerful rebuke to the hyper-masculine violence of the security forces. Their peaceful, dignified protest was impossible to portray as a riot, and it shamed the armed men in black uniforms who stood watching them.

The next day, the protest movement reached a place long considered a bastion of state support: the factory floor. Workers at some of the country's largest and most iconic state-owned enterprises—the Minsk Tractor Works, the Minsk Automobile Plant, the Belaruskali potash mines—began to walk off the job, demanding an end to the violence, the release of all detainees, and new elections. This was a critical development. The industrial proletariat, the very class the president claimed to champion, was turning against him. The high point of this workers' revolt came on August 17, when Lukashenka flew by helicopter to the Minsk Wheel Tractor Plant (MZKT) to address the workers. Instead of the deferential audience he expected, he was met with shouts of "Ukhodi!"—"Step down!" A visibly shaken president, accustomed to twenty-six years of absolute authority, was being openly heckled by his own people.

This wave of popular revulsion culminated on Sunday, August 16, with the "March for Freedom." An enormous river of people, estimated by independent media to be well over 200,000, flowed into the center of Minsk. It was the largest public gathering in the history of Belarus. The dominant color was not the red and green of the official flag, but the white, red, and white of the historical national banner, which had been transformed overnight from a fringe opposition symbol into the undisputed flag of the popular uprising. Similar massive marches took place in Grodno, Brest, Gomel, and virtually every other city in the country. A nation that had been defined by its perceived passivity had awakened, and its people were peacefully, joyfully, and defiantly demanding to be heard.

For a brief period, it seemed as though the sheer scale of the popular movement might force the regime to crumble. But the state, after a moment of hesitation, regrouped and began to fight back. The strategy shifted from indiscriminate street violence to a more targeted campaign of repression. The opposition, seeking to create a body for a peaceful transition of power, formed a Coordination Council. The authorities responded by designating it an illegal attempt to seize power. One by one, its leaders were arrested or forced to flee the country. Sviatlana Tsikhanouskaya had already been coerced into leaving for Lithuania in the first days after the election. Maria Kalesnikava, one of the last of the "trio" remaining in the country, was abducted by security services in early September. When they tried to forcibly deport her to Ukraine, she famously thwarted them by ripping up her passport at the border crossing. She was subsequently imprisoned.

Despite the repression, the massive Sunday marches continued through the autumn, a weekly festival of defiance. But the security forces grew more organized and ruthless. They began to employ tactics of mass, preemptive arrests, sealing off city centers and hunting down protesters in residential courtyards. The protests began to shrink as the personal risk of participation grew ever higher.

A final, tragic symbol of this period came in November. Raman Bandarenka, a 31-year-old artist, was detained in his own courtyard in Minsk after confronting a group of masked, plainclothes men who were tearing down the white-red-white ribbons that had become a symbol of neighborhood resistance. He was taken away and delivered to a hospital a few hours later with severe head injuries from which he would die the next day. His death, widely blamed on security forces, sent a fresh wave of grief and anger through the country, but it also underscored a grim reality. The regime was willing to use any level of violence to maintain its grip on power. The great, festive summer of awakening was giving way to a long, cold winter of repression.

CHAPTER TWENTY-FOUR: The Aftermath: Repression and International Isolation

The great, festive marches of the summer of 2020, with their seas of white-red-white flags and their euphoric sense of collective awakening, did not survive the first frosts of autumn. The movement that had brought hundreds of thousands onto the streets, powered by a shared revulsion at state violence and electoral fraud, was not defeated in a single, climactic battle. Instead, it was systematically and methodically dismantled over the months that followed, ground down by a state machine that responded to the popular uprising with a cold, bureaucratic, and utterly ruthless campaign of repression. The aftermath of the nation's awakening was not the new dawn many had hoped for, but a long, grim political winter, a period that would see the last vestiges of independent public life frozen solid and the country plunged into a deeper international isolation than at any point since the fall of the Soviet Union.

The state's strategy shifted from the chaotic street violence of the first post-election nights to a more calculated and comprehensive purge. The legal system itself was repurposed into an instrument of suppression. The rubber-stamp parliament passed a raft of new laws and amended existing ones to create a legal minefield for any form of dissent. The definition of "extremism" was expanded to be so broad as to be practically meaningless, capable of encompassing everything from subscribing to a particular Telegram channel to displaying a historical flag. Attending an "unauthorized mass event" became a serious criminal offense, as did "insulting the president" or other government officials. The legal framework was re-engineered to make any activity outside the absolute control of the state a potential crime.

The enforcement of this new reality fell to a revitalized and empowered security apparatus. The KGB, which proudly retained its Soviet name and methods, worked alongside the Ministry of Internal Affairs' Main Directorate for Combating Organized Crime and Corruption (GUBOPiK), a notoriously brutal agency that became the public face of the crackdown. Their methods were a blend of old-school terror and modern digital surveillance. They hunted down protesters by meticulously analyzing video footage from the summer marches and using facial recognition software. Raids on the homes of suspected activists became a daily occurrence, often conducted by masked men in unmarked vans who would smash down doors in pre-dawn hours.

A particularly cruel and effective tactic was the production of "repentance videos." After being arrested and often beaten, individuals would be forced to appear on camera, looking disheveled and demoralized, to confess to their "crimes"—such as participating in a protest or writing a critical comment online—and to renounce their views. These videos were then widely circulated on state-affiliated Telegram channels, a form of public humiliation designed to break the spirit of the opposition and create an atmosphere of pervasive fear and mistrust. By 2022, human rights organizations had recognized over 1,500 people as political prisoners, though the true number of those prosecuted on political grounds was believed to be many times higher. The prison system swelled with a new generation of inmates: students, doctors, musicians, factory workers, and IT professionals, their lives derailed for a single act of defiance.

With the street protests suppressed, the regime turned its attention to eradicating the entire ecosystem of independent life that had been allowed to develop over the previous decades. The next target was civil society. In a coordinated blitz that began in the summer of 2021, the Ministry of Justice went on a liquidation spree, shutting down virtually every non-governmental organization in the country. The purge was sweeping and indiscriminate. It targeted human rights groups, such as the venerable Viasna Human Rights Centre, whose leader, the future Nobel Peace Prize laureate Ales Bialiatski, was once again imprisoned. But it also dissolved environmental charities, cultural societies, organizations for the disabled, and even a bird-watching association. The goal was to create a social desert, to eliminate any form of independent organization and ensure that the only legal way for citizens to associate with one another was under the direct control of the state.

At the same time, the authorities launched a final, decisive assault on the remnants of the free press. Independent media had been a persistent thorn in the side of the government for years, but in the wake of the 2020 protests, they were reclassified as a fundamental threat to national security. The country's largest and most popular independent news portal, TUT.BY, a widely respected source of information for millions, was stormed by financial police in May 2021. Its offices were raided, its top editors arrested, and its website blocked, effectively silencing the most powerful non-state voice in the country. Nasha Niva, the oldest Belarusian-language newspaper, founded during the national revival of the early 20th century, met a similar fate, its editors imprisoned and its operations forced into exile. Scores of regional news sites were blocked, and the accreditation of all foreign journalists was revoked. The information space was systematically purged, leaving citizens with a stark choice between the shrill propaganda of state television and the exiled, "extremist"-labeled media accessible only via VPNs and Telegram.

This brutal internal consolidation had immediate and severe international consequences. The West, which had been cautiously re-engaging with Minsk in the years before the election, responded with unified condemnation. The United States, the European Union, the United Kingdom, and Canada refused to recognize the official election results and declared Alexander Lukashenka an illegitimate ruler. A series of escalating sanctions were imposed, targeting not only high-ranking officials responsible for the repression but also the economic pillars of the regime. Key state-owned enterprises, such as the potash giant Belaruskali and the oil conglomerate Belneftekhim, which were crucial sources of foreign currency, were hit with sectoral sanctions designed to cripple their ability to trade on international markets.

Any remaining illusions about the possibility of a diplomatic resolution were shattered on May 23, 2021, in an act of state-sponsored air piracy that shocked the world. Ryanair Flight 4978, traveling from Athens to Vilnius, was passing through Belarusian airspace when the pilots were contacted by air traffic control in Minsk. They were informed of a supposed bomb threat on board and were "recommended" to divert and land in the Belarusian capital. A Belarusian MiG-29 fighter jet was scrambled to escort the civilian airliner. Once the plane was on the ground, no bomb was found. Instead, security forces boarded the aircraft and arrested a single passenger: Raman Pratasevich, a 26-year-old exiled journalist and co-founder of the NEXTA Telegram channel, which had played a crucial role in coordinating the 2020 protests. His Russian girlfriend, Sofia Sapega, was also detained.

The international outrage was swift and furious. The forced diversion of a European passenger jet flying between two EU capitals was condemned as an unprecedented act of state-sponsored hijacking. In response, the EU and other Western nations banned Belarusian national airlines from their airspace and airports and advised their own carriers to avoid flying over Belarus. In a matter of days, the country was transformed into a virtual no-fly zone, its air links to the West severed, a physical manifestation of its profound political isolation.

Pushed into a corner by the West, Lukashenka lunged decisively into the embrace of his only remaining powerful ally: Russia. The Kremlin, which had watched the popular uprising in Minsk with deep alarm, saw an opportunity to turn Belarus's isolation to its strategic advantage. Vladimir Putin offered Lukashenka his full political and financial support, providing billions of dollars in loans to stabilize the Belarusian economy as it buckled under the weight of Western sanctions. In return for this lifeline, Moscow demanded what it had long sought: "deeper integration." The vague and long-dormant Union State treaty was dusted off, and a series of 28 "road maps" for economic integration were hastily approved. The rhetoric of a multi-vector foreign policy was abandoned. Minsk was now bound to Moscow more tightly than ever before, its room for diplomatic maneuver all but eliminated.

This new, subordinate relationship was underscored by a dramatic increase in military cooperation. A series of large-scale joint military exercises, such as Zapad-2021, were held on Belarusian territory, their scale and nature appearing less like a partnership and more like the Russian military establishing a new forward operating base. The Kremlin's support came at the price of Belarus's strategic autonomy.

Emboldened by Moscow's backing and eager to lash out at the European Union for the sanctions, the Belarusian government allegedly engineered a new kind of crisis in the summer and autumn of 2021. European officials accused Minsk of engaging in "hybrid warfare" by orchestrating a migrant crisis on the EU's eastern border. Thousands of people from Iraq, Syria, and other parts of the Middle East and Africa were reportedly lured to Minsk with promises of easy passage into Europe. State-run travel agencies arranged tourist visas and flights, and upon arrival, the migrants were systematically transported by Belarusian security forces to the borders with Poland, Lithuania, and Latvia and forced to cross through the forests. The result was a tense and dangerous standoff. Poland declared a state of emergency, deploying thousands of troops to the border and building a fortified wall. A tragic humanitarian crisis unfolded in the freezing forests, with thousands of desperate people trapped between Polish guards who would not let them in and Belarusian guards who would not let them go back.

The final acts in the drama of Belarus's subjugation and isolation were directly linked to the Kremlin's wider geopolitical ambitions. In February 2022, Lukashenka held another referendum, this time on a new constitution. The official results, announced with the usual implausible margins, approved a document that created a new, vaguely defined supreme body of power called the All-Belarusian People's Assembly, seen by many as a vehicle for Lukashenka to retain power in a new capacity should he ever leave the presidency. Far more consequentially, the new constitution removed the clause that had enshrined the country's status as a non-nuclear territory, a clear gesture to Moscow.

The true significance of this military alignment became terrifyingly clear just days after the referendum. On February 24, 2022, Vladimir Putin announced a "special military operation" and launched a full-scale invasion of Ukraine. A key axis of this invasion came from the north, as Russian troops that had been stationed in Belarus for "military exercises" poured across the border, launching a lightning assault toward the Ukrainian capital, Kyiv. Belarus was not a direct combatant, but it had become an indispensable staging ground, a logistics hub, and a launchpad for Russian missiles.

This complicity in the invasion sealed the country's fate. It was now seen by the West not just as a dictatorship, but as a co-aggressor in the largest European war since 1945. A new, even more punishing wave of sanctions was imposed, targeting Belarus as deeply as Russia itself. The long process that had begun with a stolen election had culminated in the nation being used as a pawn in a major war, its sovereignty effectively leased to a foreign power.

While the state celebrated its Pyrrhic victory over its own people, a new nation was being forged in exile. The repression triggered a mass exodus, the largest brain drain in the country's history. Tens of thousands of IT professionals, doctors, journalists, artists, and activists fled the country, creating large and vibrant new diaspora communities in Vilnius, Warsaw, and other European cities. This new generation of exiles, led by the internationally recognized figure of Sviatlana Tsikhanouskaya and her government-in-exile, worked to keep the dream of a democratic Belarus alive. Inside the country, resistance had not been entirely extinguished. It had simply gone deep underground, manifesting in quiet acts of sabotage, such as the "railway partisans" who disrupted tracks carrying Russian military equipment, and the vast, invisible network of citizens who continued to share information and support the families of political prisoners, a silent, atomized opposition waiting for the long winter to end.

CHAPTER TWENTY-FIVE: Belarus at a Crossroads: Challenges and Future Prospects

To arrive in Belarus in the middle of the 2020s is to arrive in a land holding its breath. The great, convulsive awakening of 2020 has passed, leaving behind a society profoundly and perhaps permanently altered, yet governed by a state determined to pretend that nothing has changed. The outward-facing image is one of rigid, Soviet-style order. The streets of Minsk are meticulously clean, the red-and-green state flags hang from every lamppost, and the machinery of government grinds on. But beneath this brittle surface lies a nation at a series of profound and perilous crossroads, its future path contingent on questions of sovereignty, succession, and identity for which there are no simple answers.

The most fundamental of these crossroads concerns the very meaning of Belarusian independence. For three decades, the country's foreign policy was a nimble, if cynical, balancing act between East and West. That era is definitively over. By serving as a staging ground for Russia's 2022 invasion of Ukraine, Minsk torched its last bridges to the West and chained its fate to that of the Kremlin. This dependency is no longer just a matter of cheap gas and fraternal rhetoric; it is a deep, structural, and military reality.

The permanent presence of Russian troops, once limited to two small Soviet-era facilities, has become a fixture of the strategic landscape. Regular and large-scale joint military exercises, like the "Zapad" series, function as a mechanism for the continuous rotation and deployment of Russian forces on Belarusian soil. The December 2024 signing of a mutual security guarantee treaty and the deployment of Russian tactical nuclear weapons have folded Belarus into Moscow's military planning and nuclear umbrella. The country has become, in effect, a forward military district of the Russian Federation, its territory a crucial buffer and potential launchpad for the Kremlin's confrontations with NATO. This de facto military integration raises the ultimate question: can a nation that has surrendered control over who carries weapons on its soil truly be called sovereign?

This military subjugation is mirrored by an economic stranglehold. The punishing Western sanctions, imposed in waves since 2020, have severed Belarus from its traditional European markets and cut off access to Western technology and finance. Key export industries, particularly potash and oil refining, have been crippled. The once-booming IT sector, a rare engine of modern, private-sector growth, has been gutted by a mass exodus of talent. The result has been a forced reorientation of the entire economy eastward. Russia now accounts for the lion's share of Belarusian trade, with China a distant second.

This dependency is a double-edged sword. While loans from Moscow and access to the Russian market have kept the unreformed, state-dominated economy from outright collapse, they have also made it a hostage to the fortunes of its patron. The "Belarusian model," once touted as an island of stability, now appears more like a stagnant pond, its future dictated by the demand for its trucks and tractors in a single, volatile market and the political whims of its creditors in the Kremlin. The long-term prospects for growth in a country isolated from global finance and technology appear bleak. The government admits that 2025 will be "much more difficult" as the full impact of sanctions takes hold.

Internally, the country faces the challenge of a society cleaved in two. The state, through its vast security apparatus, has succeeded in crushing all forms of open dissent. The political landscape has been sterilized; all genuine opposition parties and nearly two thousand non-governmental organizations have been liquidated, their leaders either imprisoned or in exile. The information space is a tightly controlled duopoly of state propaganda and officially designated "extremist" media. Yet this enforced silence does not signify consent.

The events of 2020 revealed a deep and widespread desire for political change and a modern, European identity. While the regime has managed to suppress the expression of these desires, it has done little to erase them. The generation that came of age during the protests was not defeated ideologically; it was beaten into submission or exile. This creates a society living with a deep internal schism. On one side are those who remain tethered to the state, either through genuine loyalty, fear, or economic dependency. On the other is a vast, silent, and atomized population that has lost all faith in the legitimacy of its rulers. This deep societal trauma, a collective experience of hope violently crushed, will shape the country's social and political dynamics for a generation to come.

Complicating this internal picture is the demographic crisis accelerated by the post-2020 exodus. Hundreds of thousands of Belarusians, a significant percentage of the country's workforce, have fled the country. This is not a random sample of the population; it is disproportionately young, educated, and skilled. The country has been hemorrhaging its most dynamic human capital—its software developers, doctors, entrepreneurs, and artists. The long-term economic consequences of this brain drain are severe, creating critical labor shortages and stifling innovation. The social consequences are just as profound. An entire active and engaged segment of the nation now lives outside its borders.

This has given rise to a new and powerful political phenomenon: the Belarusian diaspora. Centered in the neighboring capitals of Vilnius and Warsaw, this community of exiles is unlike any that preceded it. It is large, politically organized, and digitally connected. Through institutions like Sviatlana Tsikhanouskaya's United Transitional Cabinet and a network of media outlets and charitable foundations, the diaspora works to function as a state-in-waiting. They lobby Western governments for continued sanctions and support, provide financial aid to the families of political prisoners, and maintain a vibrant cultural and informational space that serves as an alternative to the state-controlled reality back home. Their existence poses a unique challenge for the future: how can this transnational nation, split between a suppressed population at home and an active community abroad, be re-united? Can a government-in-exile maintain its relevance and legitimacy when separated from the people it claims to represent?

Looming over all these challenges is the ultimate political question: what comes after Lukashenka? After more than three decades in power, he has constructed a political system in which all lines of authority lead directly to him. He has avoided grooming a clear successor and has systematically purged any official who showed signs of independent ambition. The 2022 constitutional reforms created a new body, the All-Belarusian People's Assembly, and provided legal guarantees for a former president, arrangements widely seen as an attempt to secure his own future. But they do little to solve the problem of an orderly transfer of power.

His eventual departure, whether through retirement or death, will create a power vacuum of immense proportions. The regime itself is likely to splinter, with factions within the powerful security services—the army, the KGB, and the Ministry of Internal Affairs—vying for control against the civilian bureaucracy. In such a scenario, the Kremlin's influence would be decisive. Moscow could attempt to install its own preferred candidate, a move that would likely lead to the final absorption of Belarus into Russia, fulfilling the long-stalled ambitions of the Union State.

Alternatively, a period of instability following his departure could create an unexpected window of opportunity for change. A fracture within the elite might force one faction to seek dialogue with the democratic opposition and the West in a bid for legitimacy. The fate of the country in such a moment would depend heavily on the geopolitical climate, particularly the outcome of the war in Ukraine and the internal stability of Russia itself. A weakened Russia might lack the capacity to impose its will, potentially opening the way for a return of the democratic forces and a genuine chance to hold the free and fair elections that were stolen in 2020.

Belarus, at the end of its long and often tragic historical journey, finds itself at a defining crossroads. One path leads further into the cul-de-sac of authoritarianism and deeper into the shadow of its eastern neighbor, a path that threatens to end in the quiet disappearance of the nation as a distinct and sovereign entity. The other path, though currently blocked by a wall of repression, leads toward the vision of a democratic, independent, and European future that flickered so brightly in the summer of 2020. The history of Belarus has been a constant struggle for statehood and identity against the overwhelming pressures of more powerful neighbors. The coming years will determine whether that long struggle has reached its final, tragic conclusion, or whether a new and unforeseen chapter is yet to be written.

Printed in Dunstable, United Kingdom